scm centrebooks

Victor de Waal

What is the Church?

SCM PRESS LTD

334 01783 1

First published 1969
by SCM Press Ltd
56 Bloomsbury Street London WC1

© *SCM Press Ltd 1969*

Printed in Great Britain by
Billing & Sons Limited
Guildford and London

Contents

Acknowledgements

Some of the material in Chapters 1 and 8 was first published in an article in *Theology* for December 1968 called, 'What is Ordination?' Chapter 4 includes matter from articles in *The Franciscan* and *Church Building*. In Chapter 6 some paragraphs first appeared in my contribution, 'The Conforming Church', in L. Bright and S. Clements (editors), *The Committed Church* (London: Darton, Longman & Todd, 1966), and I am grateful for permission to use them here.

Preface: A Serious House

A book about the church cannot evade the question that is forced on Christians in a world where men must choose how to understand themselves: What is Christianity?

To suggest an answer, however provisionally, I believe that one cannot avoid beginning with a historical judgment, namely that it is possible to know important things about Jesus. At the very least, one has to acknowledge that the church which can be discerned in the earliest records that we have, shows what kind of person he must have been, and of what kind of events he was the centre. If this is denied, it is open for each man to decide for himself what Christianity means, unless he is prepared to accept everything that happens to have survived and developed to the present day. He has no criterion by which to discriminate between what is permanently valuable and what is not.

On the other hand, it is not enough to give an account of the church's venerable origins and of its historical development, or to expound the internal consistency of the ideas which underly it, without submitting these to the critique of present experience. Otherwise a doctrine of the church easily becomes purely speculative; marvellous theories may be spun around it, but these may turn out to be as pernicious as they have been inspiring. Such a doctrine will be supported by citing the church's undoubted achievements, and not least the fact that countless men and women have found in it both sanity and sanctity. But there is more than enough evidence that could be called in the contrary sense; for it might well be said by some that if ever there was a moral tale by which mankind could be warned that, if it does not take care, the best that it has can be turned to the worst, that liberty can become oppression, and the call of friendship the constraint of fear, Christianity is that tale. And what are we left with? If we have grounds for believing that the church should be the meeting place of the contemporary world with the gospel of the New Testament, then we must try to understand how it has come to be what it is today. Only so can we hope to discern where now the sources of its life can be found.

The church interprets man to himself. In Philip Larkin's words:

> A serious house on serious earth it is,
> In whose blent air all our compulsions meet,
> Are recognized, and robed as destinies.[1]

Is this understanding true? Every man must judge for himself. This book is not an apologia. If it commends itself, it is by saying, 'Be careful how you interpret the world: it *is* like that'.[2]

NOTES

1. Philip Larkin, 'Church Going' in *The Less Deceived* (Hull: The Marvell Press, 1955).
2. Erich Heller, quoted in *The Faber Book of Aphorisms* (London: 1964).

1 Legacies

On Monday morning, 17th June 1816, preceded by his butler, carrying the sword of state in token of his civil jurisdiction and accompanied by Mr Christian, Chief Justice of the Isle, to whom he had just given breakfast in the Palace, Bishop Sparke of Ely entered his cathedral for a special service. The choir sang two anthems from the Messiah, and also a new anthem composed for the occasion by Mr Skeats, the cathedral organist; the sermon was preached on the text from I Timothy, 'The law is not made for a righteous man, but for the lawless and disobedient'; the Hallelujah Chorus ended the service. From there Mr Christian and his fellow judges proceeded to the court-house, and over the next days tried seventy-five men, who in the previous month, discontented by the unemployment and near famine that followed the Napoleonic wars, had rioted, threatened the well-to-do citizens of the nearby village of Littleport and pillaged their houses, and then in Ely ransacked the premises of bakers and publicans. (It was said that the clatter at midnight was long remembered of the Vicar of Littleport's dish-covers and plate, thrown out of his windows against the stones of the graveyard.) Twenty-four men were convicted, five to be hanged, nine to be transported to Botany Bay, and the remainder gaoled. The Bishop had bills for 25s for hangman's ropes, £5 5s 0d for a cart and two horses for the condemned men (for no citizen would *lend* a cart) and 13s for a chaise for a clergyman to accompany the criminals to the gallows.

After they'd hung for a couple of hours the men were cut down and put in the coffins with the noose still round their necks; then they were carted to a room and laid in a row for people to go and have a look at them.

It is recorded that a group of men swore

over the coffins that they'd tell their children, generation after generation, about what the Bishop and the gentry had done to those Fenmen who'd only done when they were drunk what the college lads had done many a time in Cambridge without anything being done about it.[1]

Though the Bishop of Ely no longer lives in his palace and has long been stripped of his civil power, it should hardly surprise us that today few men take seriously his claim to authority as a follower and minister of Christ. And those who are Christians, as they reflect on these events, will be troubled by the thought that in comparable circumstances their Master was found, not condemning criminals, nor yet comforting them, but alongside them on the gallows.

Behind this tale, and many others like it that could be told, lies a long history of the virtual identification of the institutional church with the political order of society. It is the dark side of a story, the other face of which records the church's role in safeguarding the values of the ancient world and, through its schools and lawyers and monasteries, civilizing and cultivating Europe.

As the Roman Empire declined and ultimately collapsed, the structure of the church, the morality it professed, the education of its clergy and the skill of its monks, came to be the chief bulwarks of law and order, so that with the rise of the new nations of the Middle Ages the bishops and abbots naturally retained their leading functions. Though the popes never succeeded for long in establishing their claim to be supreme over emperors and kings, in the Papal States and in other parts of Europe, popes and many bishops were independent sovereigns; and elsewhere, too, any differentiation between church and state was unthinkable. In some fields, such as education and in the universities, and in the care of the sick, the church's control in England lasted virtually unquestioned well into the nineteenth century, and the

10

legacy of 'established' churches is still with us. On the fringes of civilization, such as the Isle of Ely, where there was no squirearchy, and which long remained the refuge of those who had fallen foul of the law, the church was left with the civil jurisdiction that it had been given centuries before.

In retrospect we can see that the union of church and society in one great Christian culture, which we call Christendom, was but one, and that a transitory, manifestation of Christianity. But what we are only just beginning to recognize is that Christendom was a whole, that the various elements that made it up were interdependent and together constituted one world view, so that we cannot hope to preserve some of these elements in isolation from the others. We cannot, for example, deplore the political and social implications of Christendom, and hope to continue its great tradition in the arts, in architecture, and in literature. Moreover, we have to recognize that much Christian theology took Christendom for granted, and loses its relevance and its force with the passing of this frame of reference. And this is true not only of those fields where theology is concerned with society, but also in dogmatic theology, as in the doctrine of God, which depends, much more than we have been aware, on commonly accepted images. Yet like the Dutchman van Meegeren we are largely still faking old masters instead of coming to grips, as the artists and the poets are trying to do, with the puzzling and kaleidoscopic images of our own time.

Here the theologian faces the same problem as the artist, and might take comfort from the realization that his difficulties are not peculiarly his own, but are symptoms of a widespread cultural fragmentation. To give only one example: for centuries, artists in Christian Europe found it possible to express the experience of love in its many-sided aspects by painting a Madonna and child. Here was a common image which significantly represented a common experience. Men are still capable of thinking and talking about love – they do so a great deal of the time. But the

11

image has broken. No one, at least in Europe, has succeeded in painting a good Madonna for generations. Each artist is left to invent his own images and his own language. So Harvey Cox writes of the 'death-of-God' movement, in which he sees dramatic evidence of the bankruptcy of the categories that theologians have been trying to use:

> It is more the symptom of a serious failure in theology than a contribution to the next phase. Modes of religious experience are . . . shaped by cultural patterns. When social change jars the patterns, conventional ways of experiencing the holy disappear. . . . The experience of the death of the gods, or of God, is a consequence of an abrupt transition which causes the traditional symbols to collapse, since they no longer illuminate the shifting social reality. The 'Death of God' syndrome can only occur where the controlling symbols of the culture have been more or less uncritically fused with the transcendent God.[2]

The cultural revolution in which we are living is bound to have a particular critical impact on any system of ideas that has been worked out in a previous age and has in its turn underpinned the society of those times. The problems of the church here are strictly parallel to those of other institutions whose existence depends on the acceptance of common assumptions, and on the unspoken agreement to accept certain norms, checks and balances – Parliament, for example, or the universities, both institutions which today are being fundamentally questioned from within and from without. Though we can discern the roots of this revolution several centuries back, we are still certainly only at its beginning. As far as the church is concerned, however, it is probable that much of the reorganization now being engineered, in reunion schemes for example, and in synodical government, in the deployment of the ordained ministry, and the division of dioceses, will soon appear to have taken received patterns and institutions much too much for granted.

For though the age of Christendom has ended, the church itself, considered as an institution, is still very largely what Christendom made it; its structures, its manner of life, its whole way of looking at society, were shaped by a world which is passing, and in many places has already passed, away. But Christendom has left a number of legacies. Some of these are unmistakable enough and relatively easily discounted; others, because less obvious, are more subtly pervasive.

(1) A first legacy of Christendom may be discerned in the fact that many who have long ago, and perhaps regretfully, shrugged off the claims of Christianity, still hold in great estimation the great works of art and music and architecture which it has produced. And often they have kept a residual affection for the offices and ceremonies of religion as part of a treasured and picturesque folklore. But there are also Christians who, because they regret the passing of a Europe they loved, hold all the firmer to the institutional forms of a church that was part of that Europe. For many Anglicans, in particular, the vision of an England royal, rural and religious, is slow to fade. As the reality, if it ever was one, recedes into the realms of legend, there are not lacking those who, with a skill that might be envied by the Stratford producers of Shakespeare's Histories, can conjure it up before vast audiences on great occasions in our superbly maintained cathedrals. What other church can compare with the Church of England in the pageantry of fanfare and medieval oath, of Lord Lieutenant and Lord Bishop? The church belongs to England's past, to Europe's past, a past when Archbishops, Primates of All England, mattered, as Lord High Constables and Earls Marshal and Garter King of Arms mattered then. There are perhaps still occasions when, like these, the church can express the sentiment of the nation – the hopes, still to be vindicated, of a new beginning at the Coronation of Elizabeth II, the closing of an epoch at the funeral of Winston Churchill. But the danger is that those who are involved in this splendid spectacle should take themselves too seriously and mistake the show for the reality, a danger which is all the more real because large amounts of money and much property (including beautiful

13

buildings) are involved. For ancient institutions easily succumb to the temptation to justify themselves. Instead of asking the question, 'What are the basic ideas that gave rise to these structures in former times, and how should these ideas now be expressed in forms appropriate to our own age?', it is easier to ask, 'What use can we now make of these inherited institutions?' The latter question differs subtly but fundamentally from the former, for it subjects the ideas to the institutions to which it originally gave rise, instead of the other way round. So we reach the familiar situation in which submission to, and service of, an institution takes precedence over loyalty to the principles it professes. For no one is the social and political dilemma posed by this question more acute today than for the Christian.

(2) The second legacy of Christendom is closely linked with the first. The secularization of Europe and of the Europeanized world has faced the church with two problems, which are nicely pin-pointed in the two most recent sociological studies on religion in Britain.

In his book *Religion in Secular Society*, Bryan Wilson notes 'the epiphenomenal character of religious institutions and religious thinking in contemporary society' and argues that such a society is properly called secular, where 'by secularization . . . is meant the process whereby religious thinking, practice and institutions lose social significance'. The course of modern societies is only slightly influenced by religious behaviour. 'It would require an ingenious sociological analysis to show that the development of American society was materially affected by its high rate of church-going, or that of Sweden by its very low rate.'[3]

It is this phenomenon that has led Christians to speak of a 'post-Christian era' and to find comfort in the fact that in some respects the church has been reduced to the position it was in before the conversion of the Emperor Constantine. The hoped-for corollary would be that it might again find the vigour and enthusiasm of its early days. But this ignores an important difference between the situation in the first

14

two centuries and the present day. This is that today a residual Christianity has become the folk-lore and folk-morality of millions untouched by the gospel, against which it provides, as it were, an inoculation, the dead virus preventing infection by the live. Thus David Martin writes:

Religion or 'Christianity' is *still* what unites us: the umbrella identification. Just because we are a highly differentiated society in which each group has conflicting interests and psychologies we cannot physically mix in churches (beyond a certain range of social status) and yet require the word 'Christian' and the visible symbol of the church spire to symbolize our common membership in the same society. That is why the social action of the churches must be restricted to certain agreed humane objectives which do not raise the crucial dividing issues within or outside religious bodies, or to the public rhetoric of unity and social harmony which nobody takes seriously except in relation to the disputes of other people. . . . No wonder the Crown and Christianity need to be put beyond politics, and no wonder violent reactions occur whenever Christianity steps outside either agreed humanities or ritual appeals for an end to social strife such as bishops are supposed to make every time a non-professional group endeavours to improve its position.[4]

It is in this light that we must interpret the findings of such surveys as the one which showed that, whereas the vast majority of the population are not practising Christians, in the sense of going to church, yet over ninety per cent were in favour of continuing the practice of compulsory religious instruction in the state schools.[5] In the face of this 'religion', the church can make as little headway as the British Humanist Association.

This situation is reinforced by the persisting concern of the church for the moral standards of a world which is no longer predominantly Christian, and even for societies which have never been so. It has never conceived Christian ethics as anything but the way in which all men could live in accordance with their true selves. But it was only in the era of Christendom that the church came to be in a position to *legislate* for all men, and where this is possible, Christians are still prepared to do so. In other circumstances, the church sometimes does not hesitate to act as a powerful pressure group, either overtly as in Italy in the support of a particular political party, or more subtly behind the scenes, as has happened in Britain and America. More recently, however, certainly in England, this same concern has shown itself in much healthier ways. In the suggested reform of the divorce laws, in the abolition of capital punishment, in the laws on homosexual behaviour, and on illegitimacy, the church has found ways of reasoned persuasion which have spoken to all that is best in society.

Nevertheless, generally speaking, the church still finds itself cast in a very different role to the one it fulfilled in the pre-Constantinian era. In the apostle Paul's terms, it is seen, not as proclaiming a gospel, but as the upholder of the Law. The modern world sees the church in the part of the Pharisee rather than in that of Christ. And as church-goers cannot and do not live by the Law, they are readily classed, like the Pharisees, as hypocrites – reason enough for not going to church. The clergy are on the whole honourably excepted, but at the cost of being stereotyped as the promoters of 'religion' in David Martin's meaning; and it has been not uncommon for clergy, and for their wives, to feel their individual humanity threatened by this role. They know what is expected of them in belief and moral precept, and that whatever they actually say is likely to be reinterpreted in this sense. And if they are sufficiently blunt to make re-interpretation impossible, if, for example, they speak on controversial political matters, they know the outrage that follows their trespassing outside the boundaries of 'Christianity'. No doubt this also goes far to explain why many convinced lay Christians, despite all urging to the contrary, have been so reticent in admitting their beliefs among their non-Christian contemporaries. It is not that they are ashamed of their faith, but rather that they are afraid of being type-cast in a mould in which they would not recognize themselves. In others, this same anxiety shows itself by an aggressive testifying of belief, which is frequently disproportionate to the context in which it is made, and which readily misinterprets the consequent hostility as rejection of the gospel itself.

For the manifest difference between our day and the first centuries is that the vast majority of our contemporaries, seeking a liberating gospel where they may, look anywhere but to the church, from whom only *stock* responses to the world's questions are expected. Whereas what we know of Jesus would lead us to say that *he* always gave the *un*expected answer.

(3) A third legacy of the era of Christendom ultimately presents the most serious threat to the church's future, for it aligns it consistently with all those forces which resist change in the world.

Already in the fourth century when the church was first tolerated and then officially established, the process began, which, by the Middle Ages, finally led to the virtual identification of the kingdom of God with the rule of the institutional church on earth, and to the ascription of delegated divine power to its leaders. The church, particularly in the persons of its ministers, was invested with external honours and dignity borrowed from the great of the temporal order. Bishops from early time became lords and princes and lived in palaces surrounded by courtiers. Men built great churches, magnificent chapels, dominating the towns and villages and universities, to signify that God was among them. One can see, in the old prints, how the towers and spires stand out over the towns. The kingdom was, as it were, openly, indeed brashly, set before men's eyes.

Perhaps we can still understand the intention of this. Men who knew and felt only too clearly the claims of obedience, in service and taxation, pressed on them by their temporal rulers, were presented, by analogy, with the sovereign claims of God on their allegiance. But the analogy was a perilous one. The fact that the church stepped into the vacuum left by the Roman Empire led it to structure itself, particularly in the West, on the imperial model, the Bishop of Rome succeeding to the Emperor of Rome. And his authority, and that of the bishops, came readily to be understood, not as analogous to temporal power, but as equivalent to it, and indeed as far superior, resting as it did on divine guarantees and extending to the souls of men. Thus the gospel of peace and justice to mankind became the upholding of the existing social order. It is a melancholy story, and it can be told equally of Rome and Geneva and of the England of the Acts of Uniformity. The popes and bishops and presbyteries became tyrants more fearful than any merely temporal prince, because they tyrannized, and claimed to tyrannize, by God's appointment, not only over men's bodies but over their minds as well.

The corruption of power is that those who are invested with it all but inevitably have its preservation as their first concern. And this means that they will instinctively oppose any change in the circumstances that have given them this power. Thus, in the nineteenth century, the papacy advanced the strongest religious arguments in its fight to retain the Papal States, and, on a smaller scale, those bishops have been rare indeed who have willingly subdivided their dioceses. Indeed there can be few instances in which the church has willingly relinquished privileges, and when these have not had to be wrested from it forcibly when need required.

Paradoxically, much of the present apparent modernization of the churches, new canon law, new liturgy, new training for the ministry, is in fact conservative in intention, though of course often far from conservative in effect. The rationalizing and streamlining of inherited institutions may have as its concealed objective the better controlling of the system and the people subjected to it. The exercise of power, having abandoned the cruder sanctions of a past age, such as the penal laws and political disabilities, as being no longer efficient because no longer socially acceptable, can resort to more contemporary means of persuasion to maintain itself in being and extend its influence. The charade of consultation within a firm, and the techniques of advertising and of the sales representative in its approach to potential clients,

18

these conceal purposes of self-aggrandisement under a benevolent facade, itself the work of professional image makers and public relations consultants. It is not altogether fanciful to recognize in the churches a set of closed corporations concerned to protect their assets and to discourage controversy among their members. A modernized church in this sense, because, despite appearances to the contrary, it is really dedicated to perpetuating the power structures of the past, may be even further removed from the original ideas that gave it birth than the ramshackle edifice which it replaces. And being further removed, it is in fact less and not more adaptable to a changing world. John Hick has written:

> The churches as they now are cannot survive for very long. Nor should we work to prolong their life beyond the point at which new and more viable forms of Christian life have become apparent. Indeed what is to be feared is rather that the great churches, unadapted to the new age, *will* continue to survive – but by going culturally underground and becoming totally irrelevant to the ongoing life of mankind.[6]

One cannot help feeling that much of the church's modernization programme smacks of a man's putting his house in order before he dies.

NOTES

1. W. H. Barrett, *Tales from the Fens* (London: Routledge, 1963), pp. 97 f.

2. H. Cox, *On Not Leaving it to the Snake* (London: SCM Press and New York: Macmillan, 1968), p. 5.

3. Bryan Wilson, *Religion in Secular Society* (London: Watts, 1966), p. xii, p. xiv.

4. David Martin, *A Sociology of English Religion* (London: SCM Press, and New York: Basic Books, 1967), pp. 106 f.

5. Cf. *New Society*, 27th May, 1965.

6. John Hick, *Christianity at the Centre* (London: SCM Press, and New York: Morehouse-Barlow, 1968), p. 78.

2 The Hidden Kingdom

In his Reith Lecures for 1967, Edmund Leach said:

> One of our fundamental troubles is that we . . . take it for granted that there is something intrinsically virtuous and natural about law and order. It is this expectation of orderliness which generates our fear of anarchy and which thus, in a world of accelerating change, creates a panic feeling that things have got out of control. But if we are logical it would be order, not chaos, which would now fill us with alarm. An orderly world is a world governed by precedent and experience, nicely organized to cope with facts which we already know. That would be fine in conditions of technical stagnation, but in the context of a technological revolution, orderliness is simply a marker of how far the members of society have got out of touch with what is really going on.[1]

What is here written of Britain in the 1960's has a much wider cultural reference and, if the argument of the last chapter has any force, certainly applies to the church, which, not unnaturally, Edmund Leach elsewhere includes among the forces of reaction. For man and his social institutions, as for the great evolving world of nature, to look back is death. In both cases their fantastic and complex history is but the raw material for the future. The tendency that we have to make order of the past, to arrange our world tidily and safely, to think that we know what the nature of things is, what man is, what natural law is, is, strictly speaking, deadly. For the sense of security that this gives us is false. All it does is to leave us unprepared, not least morally unprepared, for what happens next. Hence comes our astonishing capacity to pretend to one another that entirely new problems do not confront us, our readiness to bring out

20

answers which are not even those that were given to older problems when they arose, but are what we succeeded in working out *after* the event.

What made Christianity originally, and Marxism, and the experimental approach to knowledge of the natural world, vivifying to man was their element of *discontinuity* with the past. Thus the apostle Paul speaks of forgetting what is behind him, and reaching out for that which lies ahead (Phil. 3.13). It is the breaking of the deadly circle of the certain and known that makes new life possible. This explains the centrality in the New Testament of the idea of liberation and forgiveness.

As far as Christianity is concerned, it is the potential of man, in himself and in community, that is the measure and judge of the present. It is not what man has been, but what he hopes to become and to be capable of that is vital. In this sense the final end judges the here and now, and man lives under the challenge of the Last Judgment. If we recognize this, we shall speak less confidently of man's nature and of his capacity for good and for evil as something immutable which prejudges any possible action – in the economic and political ordering of society, for example, or in the life of the family, or in matters of human sexuality. Nor will we be surprised at man's manifestations of hitherto unsuspected greatness or depravity.

Does this mean that we have no absolute criteria by which to determine what is good? Can we not differentiate, for example, between the intoxication of belonging to the Hitler Youth and the dedication of the Society of Friends? How are we to use the technological skills by whose means we are, or soon shall be, capable of determining the future of our world? It is inevitable that here choices have to be made, that here, as Edmund Leach in the same lectures so forcibly argued, we have the freedom and the daunting responsibility to decide our future. And in so far as the brief epoch of recorded history can help us to determine what has and what has not been conducive to human felicity, the possibility, among others, presented by Jesus of Nazareth is open to us.

In a typical incident in Charles Schulz's strip-cartoon 'Peanuts', Lucy shouts, 'Do you understand?' The little boy put his hands over his ears. 'Yes. I understand! You don't have to yell at me!' Lucy reflects. 'Perhaps you're right . . . perhaps I shouldn't yell at you so much, but I feel that if I talked to you quietly as I am doing now . . .' (and again she shouts) 'you'd never listen!' Christopher Driver, writing in *The Guardian*, commented:

> The church, of course, has always deeply distrusted Jesus's reprehensible affection for parables. Its instinct (read any papal encyclical, listen to any Billy Graham campaign) has always been to lay the 'truth' on the line and turn up the volume. . . . But as any serious artist knows, the truth then ceases to be the truth. By being too accessible, it pierces no resistance, evokes no discernment. 'Christianity,' wrote Kierkegaard, 'by becoming a direct communication, is altogether destroyed. It becomes a superficial thing, capable neither of inflicting deep wounds, nor of healing them.'[2]

The church that we know, and of which we have been speaking, is well characterized in the first half of that comment. Over the centuries its perennial instinct has been to try to tame the gospel and to contain God in its own categories. It has acted as if it knew exactly who Jesus was, has codified his teaching, and parcelled out his powers among its officials, while to the laity it has held out mainly his example of faithful obedience.

Yet, if we may judge by the New Testament, itself the product of the first communities that sprang up in response to him, the original impact of Jesus was quite other. He puzzled men and profoundly enlightened them in turn. He aroused passionate loyalties and equally passionate enmity. He refused all titles and designations – even to be called good (Mark 10.18) – and apparently would only speak of himself obscurely as the 'Son of Man'. He did not fit into any pre-existent category, and it was only in the teeth of a still unconvinced Judaism that his followers succeeded in fixing on him the label of 'Christ'. In the words that Christopher Driver uses to speak of the truth remaining the truth, he never became 'too accessible'. It is a characteristic of Jesus that persists into the resurrection appearances recorded at the end of the story. But it is expressed throughout the New Testament writings, in the parables, in the 'signs', as the Fourth Gospel calls the miracles, above all in the recurrent paradoxes – the secret *messiah*, the master washing his slaves' feet, the shepherd who is himself the sacrificially slaughtered lamb, the healer himself in need of healing, above all the king reigning from the gallows.[3] All these turn our values upside down.

Was Jesus, then, a revolutionary, as nowadays some want to say? He certainly disclaimed being the sort of revolutionary *messiah* many people at the time were hoping for and wanted him to be – a political leader who would overthrow the Roman occupation of his country and restore a free and sovereign Israel. Though, following John the Baptist, he stood in the tradition of the Hebrew prophets, critical of the existing social order, he did not use his gifts for economic and social reform either; in one parable he even seems to commend sharp business practice. We do not find him denouncing poverty or unemployment, or slavery. He seems to accept the social institutions and the judicial system of his day – even when it unjustly condemns himself.[4]

And yet in a profounder way, he is more radical than any political revolutionary, and it is not long before his followers also are accused of overturning the world (Acts 17.6). What he does is to put a question mark against all the structures of this world, against all its social and political and economic orders. He seems to accept them only provisionally and to display a royal freedom towards them. Though he respects marriage, he remains unmarried himself and says that there will be no marriage in the resurrection; though he worships in the Temple, he foretells its overthrow, and teaches that all true worship is in the Spirit; though he accepts taxation, he owns no property and scorns

23

what seems the common prudence that provides for the morrow; he submits to the Law, but himself judges no man and likewise forbids his followers to do so; he acts and teaches the refusal to oppose evil with force, and forgives his enemies.[5]

Here again is paradox. But its meaning for the first Christians was clear. In this sitting lightly to all the world's categories and values, in this authoritative freedom to reinterpret them, making low high and high low, they discerned God's own sovereignty over the societies and cultures of mankind. None have permanence or a final binding authority. They knew Jesus as a man who walked the earth, and they looked to him as Lord, looked *forward* to him as the final arbiter of men and history.[6]

For the clue to the resolution of these paradoxes is to be found in the fact that the distinctive perspective of the first Christians was *forwards* into the future. We, whose typical outlook as Christians, is, on the contrary, backwards into history, are frequently puzzled by the fact that the New Testament does not tell us more about the person, the personality, and the biography of Jesus. Much that we would like to know, and which the first disciples must surely have known, is simply not recorded. The fact is that the early church saw Jesus' coming as having only just begun; his own life until his crucifixion, their own life now, transformed as they believed by his Spirit, were a foretaste only, an earnest of the final reordering of the whole world. The kingdom he had inaugurated was like a seed growing secretly, we know not how, towards the harvest; it was like the leaven interiorly leavening the whole lump. When all was renewed, all recreated, *then* they would see him as he is and share in his glory. But *now* was the time of paradox, and of revolutionary songs which tell of the ultimate downfall of the proud and the rich, and of the exaltation of the humble and meek.[7]

Here was the liberation of the gospel, the secret of its undiminished freshness, the reason why it transcended the

24

culture of its first preaching and has remained immensely attractive to many who have been alienated (who will say it is their fault?) from the Christian tradition. For if in Christ's person and action greatness was revalued as humility, power as service, justice as forgiveness, prudence as self-abandonment, love of life as a readiness to lose it; if the glory of God was to be seen above all in the cross of Jesus Christ, then the means of transforming their life in the world was within the grasp of all men. For it was to the experience of ordinary men that Jesus spoke when he blessed the poor and the sorrowful, the oppressed and the hungry for righteousness, and promised them the inheritance of earth and of heaven.[8]

If, then, one were to put the question, 'What is the Church?' to the first generation of Christians, they would not conceive of an answer in terms of a settled and ordered social organization like any other in the world. Hence the impossibility of finding patterns there for later church order. What they do is to borrow, and adapt in haste, appropriate images from the Old Testament, and also from the Hellenistic world, and this to describe three connected realities.

The first is Jesus himself as they have known him. Because they saw the promises to Abraham, the covenant with Moses, the faithful Remnant of which the prophets speak – all of which Israel only imperfectly realized – perfectly fulfilled in him, the first Christians, as it were, narrowed down into one man, Jesus, the whole call and providence of God and the whole response of man, of which their religious tradition spoke. He is the seed in whom all nations of the world shall be blessed; he is the new Moses; he is Israel with whom the covenant is unbreakably made; the Vine that bears fruit; the Davidic King triumphing over all his enemies; the Good Shepherd who gathers the scattered sheep; the cornerstone of the new Temple, or, alternatively, the Temple itself in which God dwells and in which true worship is offered; the last single remnant of the true Israel (as Mark pictures him in the Passion); the Suffering

25

Servant of God who is to be a Light to the nations; the Son of Man of Daniel's vision gloriously ascending to the Father. More, he is a Second Adam, the new and unfailing bearer of God's image, in whom all mankind is potentially recreated.

The second reality is one of hope, a dream of the end when 'God will be all in all' (I Cor. 15.28). Here the same images are ascribed to the church, but seen now as the spotless bride united to Christ the Bridegroom, the holy city, new Jerusalem, coming down out of heaven. For he who, in his exaltation on the Cross, drew all men to himself has made all things new and all who participate in his body are made 'a kingdom, priests to his God and Father' (Rev. 1.6). The grain of wheat that fell into the ground and died has borne much fruit.

The third reality is the small and scattered communities of disciples round the Mediterranean Sea. To them also the images apply, but only in the interim, only proleptically. The church now is a sign of the kingdom, a sacrament of the world to come. Christians are the pilgrim people of God, feeding on the manna of his flesh, living stones of a Temple still in the building, soldiers in a war not yet finally won, athletes in training for a prize not yet achieved. They are the citizens of the new Jerusalem, the city set on a hill, the first-fruits of the harvest, and in and through them the leaven and salt are at work in the world.[9]

Because they believed their universe to be under imminent judgment and in the process of secret transformation, the early Christians could accept its categories and institutions provisionally, and keep them in perspective. The fact that in the first instance this perspective was foreshortened – the transformation was expected to be completed in the lifetime of the first generation of disciples, the coming of Jesus in glory was daily awaited, an expectation due to be disappointed – is less important than the existence of the perspective itself. Thus an anonymous Christian wrote in about AD 130 in the *Epistle to Diognetus*:

26

> Christians are not distinguished from the rest of mankind either in locality or in speech or in customs. For they dwell not somewhere in cities of their own, neither do they use some different language, nor practise an extraordinary kind of life. . . . They dwell in their own country but only as sojourners: they bear their share in all things as citizens, and they endure all hardships as strangers. Every foreign country is a fatherland to them, and every fatherland is foreign. . . . They obey the established laws, and they surpass the laws in their own lives. . . . Their existence is on earth, but their citizenship is in heaven.[10]

Christians did not withdraw from the world, though this has always been a temptation; on the contrary they were diligent, paid their taxes, and obeyed the civil ruler.[11] But they sat lightly to it. This accounts for the ethic of urgency in the earlier epistles – there is hardly time to devote oneself to marriage or worldly affairs – an ethic that was later in more settled circumstances to be misinterpreted in a puritan sense.[12]

Thus we can also understand the early church's apparent acquiescence in slavery. The first Christians did not accept slavery because, initially, they were a tiny group powerless to change it, nor did they subscribe to that larger pietistic irresponsibility which believed that all would be set right 'in the after-life'. Nor, like a later Protestant ethic, did they draw a firm boundary between the sacred and the secular, making allegiance to God only a matter of interior religion, and letting the world operate according to its own laws; a view which led, as some historians have argued, to the rise of capitalism, when employers of highest individual Christian principles found it possible to treat human beings as 'labour', that is, as one impersonal economic factor among others.

Initially, they took the world as it was because they saw it virtually at an end:

> The Christ, in their expectation, was the one through whom God would create a new order, or a new humanity. Through their life together in the Christian community they experienced its blessings so compellingly that they found it hard to believe that the old evil order could possibly last much longer.[13]

27

Though, in the event, the church had to accept that the end was to be delayed,[14] it maintained its stance. It stood, as it were, askew to the world, and accepted it only critically. For already the good news was being announced to the poor, already the release of prisoners and the recovery of sight for the blind was being proclaimed, and liberation to the oppressed (Luke 4.18). The world was being transformed, and Christians felt themselves to be participating in the process of transformation.

It has been argued with some plausibility that it is those societies which have their roots in Christianity, even if their Christianity has been secularized in liberal or Marxist forms, which are prepared to make the attempt to change themselves for the better – unlike most cultures of the East, which are still bound by a deep conviction of the unchanging and unchangeable nature of things.

NOTES

1. Edmund Leach, *A Runaway World?* (London: BBC, 1968), pp. 9 f.

2. Christopher Driver reviewing Robert Short, *The Gospel according to Peanuts* (Richmond, Va.: John Knox Press, and London: Fontana, 1966) in *The Guardian*, 17th March, 1966.

3. Cf. e.g. Mark 1.44; Luke 4.23; John 10.11 ff.; 13.1–17; 19.19, 36.

4. Cf. e.g. Matt. 20.1 ff.; Mark 14.7; Luke 16.1 ff.; 17.7 ff.; John 6.15.

5. Cf. e.g. Matt. 5.39; 6.34; 7.1; 8.11, 20; 26.52; Mark 10.6–9; 11.17; 12.17, 25; 13.2; 14.64; Luke 23.34; John 2.1 ff.; 4.24; 8.11; 12.47.

6. This whole section owes much to Karl Barth's *Church Dogmatics*, IV.2 (ET, Edinburgh: T. & T. Clark, 1958), pp. 171 ff.

7. Cf. Matt. 6.10; 13.33; Mark 1.15; 4.26 ff.; Luke 1.46 ff.; 11.20; Rom. 18.18 ff.; II Cor. 1.22; I John 3.2; Rev. 1.7.

8. Cf. Matt. 5.3 ff.; Luke 6.20 ff.

9. A full list of references is impossible, but the reader can follow them in a concordance. Here is a selection: Gen. 22.18; Ex. 24.8; Deut. 18.15; Ps. 118.22; Isa. 4.11; 5.1 ff.; 11.11; 42.1–7; 49.6; 53; Ezek. 34.1 ff.; Dan. 7.13 f.; Matt. 5.13 f.; 8.17; 21.33, 42; Mark 11.10; 14.50, 62; Luke 2.32; 3.38; John 2.21; 6.48 ff.; 10.11 ff.; 12.24, 32; 15.1 ff.; Acts 2.1 ff., the first fruits were presented at Pentecost; 3.22, 25; 4.11; 7.37; 13.47; 26.23; 1 Cor. 3.9, 11, 16; 12.27; 15.45 ff.; Gal. 3.16; 4.26; Eph. 2.19–22; 5.23 ff.; 6.11 ff.; II Tim. 2.3 ff.; Heb. 1.3; I Peter 2.5–9, 22 ff.; Rev. 21.2 ff., 22.

10. *Epistle to Diognetus*, v.

11. Rom. 13.1–7; II Thess. 3.6–13; I Peter 2.13–17.

12. Cf. Rom. 13.11 ff.

13. T. G. A. Baker, *What is the New Testament?* (London: SCM Press, and New York: Morehouse-Barlow, 1969), pp. 17f.

14. Cf. II Peter 3.8 f.

3 Water and the Holy Spirit

At Sandringham Parish Church in Norfolk a visitor may see considerable evidence both of royal piety and of piety towards royalty. There is the solid silver altar, presented by Mr Rodman Wanamaker, an admiring American millionaire, to Queen Alexandra in memory of King Edward VII. On its front is embossed the royal coat of arms, suitably supported in this case, not by the lion and the unicorn, but by two kneeling angels. There is the pulpit, equally of silver. And there are two fonts. One is of the ninth century, a deep bath cut out of stone, brought back from Rhodes by the Victorian Duke of Edinburgh for the goldfish in the park. Rescued by the present incumbent, it now stands hard by the church, a convenient seat on which to photograph one's girl-friend. The other font is in occasional use: it stands, hung about with loyal flags, under the West Tower, guarded by St Edward the Confessor, done in stained glass after the image of the Duke of Clarence. It is in origin an elegant Florentine bird-bath.

A whole history of Western Christianity could be written between these two fonts – a history of the gradual obscuring of the most eloquent of Christian signs until, having become 'too accessible, it pierces no resistance, evokes no discernment'.[1]

To take first the old font, the one from Rhodes, typical of most fonts in the early Christian centuries, in which a grown man or woman could stand in the water. Paul wrote to the Romans:

> We died to sin: how can we live in it any longer? Have you forgotten that when we were baptized into union with Christ Jesus we were

baptized into his death? By baptism we were buried with him, and lay dead, in order that, as Christ was raised from the dead in the splendour of the Father, so also we might set our feet upon a new path of life (Rom. 6.2-4).

These words, and others that Paul wrote about the effect of becoming a Christian, become intelligible if we recall what happened at Christian baptism in his time. The baptism which those Jews practised who first accepted Jesus of Nazareth as the promised *messiah*, the Christ, was nothing new. Some Jewish sects, for example John the Baptist's, already employed baptism as a sign of renewal; and in the Dispersion outside Palestine a ritual bath was at the time the recognized way of becoming a Jew, as important as circumcision, which of course could apply only to men. Leaving aside for the moment the unconscious symbolism of the rite, rabbinic writers see the meaning of these latter baptisms of proselytes as signs both of purification and of participation by the person to be initiated in those decisive events, in which the community he is joining saw its own origins – the crossing of the Red Sea and of the Jordan at the Exodus. (The flaw in this analogy is, of course, that the whole point of the story of the Red Sea and of the Jordan is that those who crossed them did not get wet!)

Christian baptism is in origin a no doubt largely unpremeditated continuation of this accepted practice. But Paul's interpretation of what happened at this rite is new. He is concerned to emphasize that faith in Christ involves a radical renewal of man's behaviour, that the excellence of a man's moral life can stem only from his allegiance to Christ. So when, as then used to happen, the candidate for baptism is stripped of his clothes, Paul describes him as 'discarding the old nature with its deeds' (Col. 3.9).

At Jerusalem in the time of St Cyril at the end of the fourth century this was preceded and emphasized by the candidate facing West into the darkness after sunset on the night of Easter, and, stretching out his hand, repudiating Satan and his works of sin. And then, turning towards the lights of the

31

baptistery, he stepped quite naked down into the water. (For decency's sake the women were attended by deaconesses – the principal reason for the existence of that order.) Paul speaks of being buried with Christ (Rom. 6.4) – Cyril in Jerusalem can point 'over there' to the traditional place of the Lord's actual sepulchre. The waters have always stood in man's unconscious both for the womb from whence he came (who at school did not have a print on the wall of Botticelli's 'The Birth of Venus'?), and also for the grave to which he must return. Here the order is reversed, the grave becomes the prelude to resurrection. The nakedness of the candidate is more than the conventional nudity of the bath; it is the nakedness of death (as of Christ's death on the gallows) and also the nakedness of birth. We brought nothing with us, we can take nothing away with us (I Tim. 6.7) – it was insisted at baptism that even every ribbon and ring be discarded. The candidate stands in the water to confess his faith. It is doubtful if he was ever dipped right under, a dangerous proceeding; water was poured over him as he stood there, three times initially, for his Lord's three days in the tomb, three times later also for his trinitarian faith. Thus Hippolytus ordered, writing about AD 215:

Let him who baptizes lay hand on him saying thus:
'Dost thou believe in God the Father Almighty?'
And he who is being baptized shall say:

'I believe.'

Let him forthwith baptize him once, having his hand laid on his head. And after this let him say:

'Dost thou believe in Christ Jesus, the Son of God,
Who was born of Holy Spirit and the Virgin Mary,
Who was crucified in the days of Pontius Pilate,
And died,
And rose the third day living from the dead,
And ascended into the heavens,
And sat down at the right hand of the Father,
And will come to judge the living and the dead?'

And when he says: 'I believe', let him baptize him the second time. And again let him say:

'Dost thou believe in the Holy Spirit in the Holy Church,
for the resurrection of the flesh?'
And he who is being baptized shall say: 'I believe'. And so let him
baptize him the third time.[2]

Then he comes up out of the water: Paul speaks of being
'raised to life with Christ' (Eph. 2.6). Then, as always after
a bath, he is rubbed with oil: Paul speaks of being 'chris-
tened' (II Cor. 1.21–22), anointed by the same Spirit who
descended on Jesus after his own baptism in Jordan,
anointing him as *messiah*. To the candidate the voice from
heaven also speaks as it is reported to have spoken to Jesus,
'Thou art my Son' (Mark 1.11). Paul writes, 'You have
received the Spirit of adoption, whereby we cry "Father" '
(Rom. 8.15). ('The fifth-century heretic Nestorius pressed
the analogy so far as to see in *Jesus*' baptism also his adoption as Son of God.)

Then the candidate puts on clean clothes, probably white
clothes: Paul speaks of 'putting on the new nature which
shews itself in a just and devout life' (Eph. 4.24), or simply
of 'putting on Christ' (Gal. 3.27). He is brought to the
assembled church, the bishop received him by laying hands
on his head, he participates for the first time in Holy Communion: it is a foretaste of the kingdom, and there may be
an additional cup of milk and honey as a sign that he has
entered the promised land.[3]

For the Christians of the first centuries, what we separately
call the sacraments of baptism, confirmation and first communion were a unity which spoke clearly. And one can
readily imagine the impact it had on a man. The call of
Christ has touched his longing to find his real self, to be
made new. Here is a way of giving himself completely and
simply without any pretensions. And here is a way of symbolizing to him his acceptance, by God and the community,
for the person he really is, with all his roles stripped
away. He becomes a child again, with the child's honesty
and the child's trust.[4]

Such an experience cannot readily have been forgotten.

Here for each Christian, individually and in his own person, the death and resurrection of his Lord was recapitulated, to be translated now into the moral renewal of his own existence, as he 'died to sin' and 'set his feet upon a new path of life'. And here was a point to which a Christian could refer his own sufferings, his poverty and sorrows, and not least the self-denial involved in obeying the new commandment to love his neighbour with the same quality of love that God had shown to him in Jesus Christ. Here was little danger that the light burden and easy yoke of the cross would cease to be at the heart of a Christian's life. To sin seriously again was a denial of Christ, a repudiation of the community that was the sign of the world's renewal as the kingdom of God; and those who apostatized altogether were said to 'crucify the Son of God on their own account and hold him up to contempt' (Heb. 6.6). One can understand the church's constant refusal to baptize a second time, and the strictness of the penitential discipline which it reluctantly developed over the years.

Christianity inherited from Judaism the conviction that religion and ethics are one, and Paul was in the prophetic tradition of Amos when he argued with his converts that their beliefs and their behaviour were interdependent. This conviction was expressed in baptism, and, as we shall see, was central to the eucharist also. It was there in John's water-baptism of repentance, and no doubt in the baptism administered by Jesus' own disciples in his lifetime. It was implied in the metaphor of a new birth in the discourse between Jesus and Nicodemus in the Fourth Gospel, and in the clear parallel between Paul's summary of the gospel – 'Christ *died* for our sins . . . was *buried* . . . he was *raised* . . .' (1 Cor. 15.3 ff.) – and his baptismal doctrine. Again, the way in which faith and a new moral life were linked by baptism is clearly seen in the climax of Matthew's Gospel, where Jesus is represented commissioning his disciples:

All authority in heaven and on earth has been given to me. Go therefore and make disciples of all nations, baptizing them in the name of the Father and of the Son and of the Holy Spirit, teaching them to observe all that I have commanded you; and lo, I am with you always, to the close of the age (Matt. 28.18-20).

Here, typically, the church is pictured as looking forward; it is a sign of hope. The promise of the world's renewal as the kingdom, inaugurated in the person of Jesus, is established among every nation and tribe and people and tongue (Rev. 7.9). The Christian gospel claimed to point in Jesus Christ towards man's fullest potential, to illuminate and interpret his universal experience by a future reference. For the individual Christian, this belief was focused by his baptism, in which, acting it out, he expressed both his acceptance of his nature as a man, living and dying, and also his faith in the true meaning and destiny of man and nature in death and in birth.

At his baptism a man stood naked and alone. But because man is not fundamentally self-sufficient and can only become and understand himself in relationship with others, his life is necessarily a life in community. So John V. Taylor said, writing about the old culture of Africa:

As the glow of a coal depends upon its remaining in the fire, so the vitality, the psychic security, the very humanity of a man, depends on his integration into the family.[5]

As soon as he had been baptized a man was brought into the church already assembled for the eucharist. To the question, 'Dost thou believe in the Holy Spirit in the Holy Church?' he had replied, 'I believe'. For he knew that his longing for a new life could only be fulfilled in the community which gathered round Christ and lived by his Spirit. His baptism made it plain to him that more was involved than a desire on his part, more than a psychological change of attitude. The reality of the moral transformation which was happening in him was grounded on the moral integrity of Jesus his Master, who had survived even the test of death. His new life was guaranteed by the actual community of other people which he now joined and in which Jesus was

35

alive. He knew that the church was indispensable to Christian living, and that Spirit and church were inseparable.

The long and general neglect of the doctrine of the Holy Spirit is directly related to the decline of a genuinely communal life in the church. So in the popular mind the Spirit tends to be thought of on the analogy of a stimulant or a drug, to which Christians have private access, a nebulous commodity for their soul's metabolism to work on, nourishing what is called the 'spiritual life'. Such an analogy is misleading because it depersonalizes that gift of himself which is God's grace, and which Christians recognize above all in the coming of Jesus. Convinced as he was that the Spirit which vivified the Christian communities was the Spirit of Christ, Paul, while conceding the possibility of private gifts such as 'speaking in tongues', put all his emphasis on those moral gifts that build up the community, that promote justice and peace and reconciliation, the qualities of Jesus himself. The fruit of the Spirit is above all charity, then joy, peace, patience, kindness, goodness, fidelity, gentleness, self-control. [6]

Two things make a human being, reason and love: the ability to order the world, to understand it, the capacity for truth, and the capacity for relationship, the fact that men discover and fulfil themselves only in community with others. These two aspects go together. In his grasp of truth, though it becomes his very own, a man is aware of his individual insufficiency, of his dependence on other people. And the quality of his relationship is in turn informed by a concern for integrity. His family, his teachers, his friends, a single person perhaps who loves him, has enabled him to be and do more than he could ever have been or done by himself. And every such group and relationship is more than the sum of its constituent members, it possesses its own life, an 'esprit de corps', which gives it its distinctive quality.

The promise of Christ's Spirit is addressed precisely to these two characteristics of man, and his work is best described in *personal* terms. He is the Spirit who illumines men's minds, who enables them to see what inexplicably they have been blind to before, who brings to remembrance all that Jesus has said, by whom they may truly interpret the world and be led into all truth.[7] And his is the mutual love that informs the community of Jesus' disciples, and overflows from it, if they are expectant of his coming and open to one another. He is indeed 'esprit de corps', *the* Spirit of *the* body – the body of Christ's church.

The second font at Sandringham brings us to baptism as it is generally administered today. This will doubtlessly be done decently and in order, but the symbols are meagre, and action has largely been replaced by theological explanation. Kierkegaard's words readily again come to mind: 'a superficial thing, capable neither of inflicting deep wounds, nor of healing them'.[8] For, at the least, it now seems hardly appropriate to describe the experience of the baptized as of 'those who have been enlightened, who have tasted the heavenly gift, and have become partakers of the Holy Spirit, and have tasted the goodness of the word of God and the powers of the age to come' (Heb. 6.4–5).

Two separate issues are involved here – the long prevalence of infant baptism and the fading of the old symbols, which began as the church came to think of itself in organizational rather than sacramental terms,[9] and which has been further influenced by the modern world's separation of man from nature.

Originally, in all probability, the baptism of children of Christian families reflected nothing more, but also nothing less, than a desire that they should share from the beginning of their lives in all the privileges of the redeemed community. In such circumstances, while their actual baptism would not be even a memory to them, they would experience in the church, as they grew up, that life of the Spirit which is the continuation and working out of baptism. It is important to remember that initially they participated in the *whole* of baptism – they were also 'confirmed' and given their first communion, and would become regular communicants as soon as they were weaned. This is still the practice of the Eastern Orthodox churches. But, while infant baptism was widespread in the first three centuries, it was by no means universal. St Basil (*c.* 330–379), for example, though of devout parentage, was not baptized till adulthood.

To this desire was added, largely under the influence of St Augustine, a new motivation. As the notion of original guilt became generally accepted, it became important to baptize infants to save them from damnation if they should die prematurely. The same principle was applied at the conversion of pagan tribes: they were baptized, by force if necessary, as soon as the opportunity presented itself, for their own good. In the Middle Ages it is probable that most Christians were in fact baptized by the midwife, to be on the safe side. The results of this decline into superstition are manifest in a post-Christendom situation, where infant baptism remains a precautionary measure taken by parents who do not believe in original guilt, or damnation, or indeed in the church.

The second difficulty goes deeper. It can be put as follows.

The motto of modern European man may be said to have been written by René Descartes in 1637 – *Cogito ergo sum.* 'I think, therefore I exist.' Though nowadays philosophers argue that the inference is logically illegitimate, here nevertheless is the root of our intellectual achievement. It summarizes that attitude of reflective, critical, analytical reasoning, the scientific method, which has produced the technological revolution. We mentally separate ourselves from the rest of nature, we conceptualize the world; and so we can generalize from it, we become capable of controlling it, of 'conquering' it, as used to be said. We can do this to our own past, too. We develop what we call the historical sense. We do it to art, to literature, to poetry – we become critics. We can do it to ourselves – we become psychologists. The practical consequences of this attitude in a relatively short time have been astonishing. Experiment, invention, social mobility, these have made possible not least an increase in human dignity, for example through the control of disease and eventually perhaps of poverty as well.

But the price is heavy. Our separation from the rest of nature has increased the more we control and exploit it. A generation ago already, Aldous Huxley in *Brave New World* had a vision of synthetic food, test-tube babies and pre-packaged information. We have learned to understand much: but we have to kill in order to dissect, and it remains a question what it is that we observe when we shine a light into our unconscious, for darkness lightened is no longer darkness.

The primacy of reflection over being means that fatal hesitation that inhibits spontaneity in life as in art. Life and knowledge have reversed roles. If once men lived and learned wisdom in the process, now we are taught techniques for living in advance. A writer, an artist, an architect, well taught, will try to do the sum of all that has influenced him – to steer the all but unnavigable course between plagiarism and gimmickry. And we, like him, are self-conscious, always looking in the glass, checking on ourselves to make sure we are experiencing, functioning, enjoying ourselves, or are *with* the fashion.

This has meant also the atomizing of society, and many have discovered that individualism can also mean loneliness. Our mental hospitals are full of people who have broken under our culture's insistence on individual self-sufficiency and the constant need for personal choice and personal decision. Most paradoxically perhaps, our sexuality, which testifies precisely to our continuity with the rest of nature, and which lies at the root of all older forms of society (family, tribe, race), has become a largely undirected force. It is as often (possibly more often) destructive of human relationships and individual human happiness as it is constructive. Its only consistent use is in advertising, to help create the market needed for the perpetually expanding economy on which our wealth depends.

Western Christianity could hardly have remained immune from the tide of this civilization, or at any rate immune from its undertow. Reflecting on the celebration of Christmas, Jonathan Miller recently wrote of

the way in which the poetical part of the public soul is progressively becoming replaced by prose . . . the way in which we are less and less able to understand what is said or done to us unless we can readily translate it all into the Esperanto of common pragmatism. It is the awareness of this tendency, I am sure, which is responsible for the renewed interest in restoring ritual to the modern theatre. And yet the process has gone too far for someone like Peter Brook, for example, to be able, by a conscious effort of will, or even imagination, to graft the heart back into the corporate imagination. The whole point about ritual, with its use of formal ceremony, is that the potency of the symbols, or indeed of any hierophany, is dispersed immediately the congregation knows that it is in the presence of something being used as such.[10]

This is the dilemma of Christian worship: baptism, eucharist, prayer itself. If it is spontaneous, it will tend to be superficial and sentimental; if, on the other hand, it is theologically adequate, it will almost certainly lack spontaneity. Christians *think* of themselves making eucharist, they *think* of themselves praying. And the scholarly historical and theological work of liturgical commissions can actually aggravate matters by destroying what habits of worship are left.

The flight from images in prayer, the turning to negative theology in talking about God, in the tradition of the medieval treatise *The Cloud of Unknowing*, and the conviction of many that words are practically useless in evangelism, these are some of the reactions to be found among Christians today. But these are all essentially *non*-sacramental, and it is difficult to see how their specifically *Christian* content could be preserved. The urgency of this question is illustrated by the same reaction in the moral field, where it takes the form of a revolt against legalism – a necessary revolt, but one that can lead straight into antinomianism.

As man's education came increasingly to be designed for intellectual ends, so spontaneity and the whole range of his emotions were relegated more and more to the level of the irrational and the subhuman. His own body became a stranger to him. So the old symbols also faded, the symbols that held nature and man's mind together, and lay at the root of his communal life. And there faded with them the Christian signs, the parables that could evoke discernment in a man and drew him to put a value and a meaning on his experience. Only 'direct communication' is left, and 'Christianity, by becoming a direct communication, is altogether destroyed'.[11]

NOTES

1. Cf. p. 22.
2. Hippolytus, *Apostolic Tradition*, 21; cf. E. C. Whitaker, *Documents of the Baptismal Liturgy* (London: SPCK, 1960), pp. 5 f.
3. *ibid.* 23.
4. Cf. Mark 10.15.
5. John V. Taylor, *The Primal Vision* (London: SCM Press, 1963), p. 100.
6. Cf. I Cor. 11–14; Gal. 5.22 f.
7. Cf. John 14.26; 16.13.
8. Cf. p. 22.
9. Cf. Chapters 5 and 6.
10. *The Listener*, 19th December, 1968.
11. Cf. p. 22.

4 Bread and Wine

At the time Descartes was writing, Puritan reformers were smashing the pictures and statues with which their Christian ancestors had filled the churches. For they shared his conviction that thinking was a better guide to living than the ambiguity of parable and of the imagination. They catechized endlessly, they rewrote the liturgies as sermons, or suppressed them altogether in favour of preaching. They wrote tract upon tract, homily upon homily. And all the while, unsuspected by themselves, they possessed images none the less, only these were images of the mind, inaccessible to hammer or axe. And infinitely more dangerous. For unlike the old earthy images in which men might discern a dim reflection of God and his saints, but which even the superstitious could hardly identify with them, the images of the mind were readily confused with the reality they represented. The words of which they were made could easily be thought of as exhaustively descriptive of the truth. So when it came about that words began to fail, and these images, too, were seen to be of man's making, God seemed to die also. And the world became absurd. 'In those days there was no king in Israel; every man did what was right in his own eyes' (Judges 21.25). So the author of the Book of Judges ends, summing up before the kingdom of Saul and David brought sacred order and meaning into his society. For us the situation is reversed, the sacred order has broken, the 'king' has died, and, as the art and the literature of the last decades testifies, men live in fragile private worlds at the mercy of contradictory pressures and inspirations.

In this, the response of a new generation is the looking for

42

the lost roots of a common humanity, for a new beginning, the search for innocency, so vividly expressed in the musical *Hair*, and particularly in the song 'Where do I go?', which ends with the cast standing briefly in the half-light simple and naked on the stage. This, too, underlies the sexual revolution among the young which has little to do with a more ancient debauchery. In a world where spontaneity is consistently inhibited, making love is at a premium; and if people are hurt, that, too, is largely because we take so little trouble to educate our emotions.

Alongside the flight from images, there is to be found also among Christians this same search for a new beginning, in the hope that the process of their fading has *not* gone too far, and that it may yet be possible 'to graft the heart back into the corporate imagination'.[1] This is the hope that has motivated the liturgical movement from its beginnings in the nineteenth-century revival of sacramental practice, particularly among Roman Catholics and Anglicans; the frequent celebration of the eucharist where this had been rare, the normal receiving of communion by the laity where this has been exceptional for over a millennium. It inspired the ecclesiologists in their principles of church architecture, the ritualists in their revival of medieval ceremony, and the new church artists and musicians. And in this century the scholarly study of the liturgy, matched by popular teaching and the widespread re-ordering of worship, has been central to the life of nearly all the churches. The hope that, as the old tree is pruned, new life will rise from its roots, rests on the conviction that the Christian symbols are not the arbitrary inventions of a new religion. They are, as we saw in the case of baptism, particular forms of the universal images which arise out of man's experience of himself as part of nature and society and, in all religions, take conscious form in picture, word, or action, in response to the particular environment and historical circumstances in which men find themselves. For the Christian, *the* historical event is the death and resurrection of Jesus Christ, the event which for him reveals the hidden meaning of the images and interprets them, the event which, in the foreknowledge of God, has been their meaning from the beginning. It was towards the final revelation of this mystery that, in Christian interpretation, the writers of the Old Testament looked. They meditated on the Exodus, which for them was the constitutive event of Israel's history, and in the light of which the Jews came to understand themselves as the chosen people of God. They saw in the crossing of the waters, by which they themselves were saved and their enemies destroyed, in the trials and nourishment of their desert wanderings, in their entry into the promised land, both the recapitulation of the creation myth and the type of a new deliverance in the future.

The first Christians, writers of the New Testament and Fathers of the church, understood and proclaimed the event of Christ in the categories they had inherited from the Old Testament. In Jesus Christ the looked-for final deliverance is accomplished. In his exodus sin and the last enemy, death itself, are judged and destroyed; in him the new creation is begun as Israel is reconstituted under a new covenant.

In Jesus the images are fulfilled; but they are not abrogated. While this world lasts they remain, not shadows now of a hidden mystery, but effective signs of a mystery revealed, sacraments by which, participating in Christ's work done once for all, men may know God and truly interpret their lives. Their passing through the waters of baptism is but a likeness of Jesus' death and rising again, yet it conveys the reality of his redemption. The oblation of bread and wine, and the sharing in the eucharistic meal, are but a likeness of Jesus' perfect self-offering to the Father and an image of the messianic banquet, yet they allow men to share in the realities they signify. The Lord's Day and the festivals of the Christian year are but the commemorations of God's actions in history, yet they enable men even now, to live in the presence of those events. And the same, it may be said, is true of churches of stone. In their building is exemplified the pattern and order, the mutual coinherence of the images. They are likenesses of the church itself, the spiritual Temple, built of 'living stones' (I Peter 2.5), whose 'foundations are the apostles and prophets, Christ Jesus himself being the chief corner-stone' (Eph. 2.20). They enable the Christian people in every time and place to manifest itself for what it is, and in its worship to anticipate here and now the eternal life of God's kingdom.

We saw how for a Christian of early times his belief and his behaviour were focused in baptism – on the one hand his faith in God and in the meaning he had revealed for the world in the kingdom inaugurated by Jesus, and on, the other, the renewal of his own life and the way he would live from now on. Baptism, in which he shared in the work of God in Christ, gave direction to his life and was there to be referred to in times of hardship and temptation. This interaction of faith and practice informs the whole of Christian worship, and most particularly the eucharist, in which the community constantly renews its participation in the baptismal mystery and looks forward to the fulfilment of the kingdom.[2] Good liturgy is therefore vital to the health of Christ's body, and the obscuring of its movement and its signs correspondingly deleterious both to its life and its faith.

Paul wrote to the Romans:

Therefore, my brothers, I implore you by God's mercy, to offer your bodies a living sacrifice, holy and acceptable to God, which is your reasonable worship. (Rom. 12.1).

He uses these words, words which subsequently came to be used in Christian liturgies – 'offer a living sacrifice', 'reasonable worship' – to describe not a service in church, but the day-to-day living of his ordinary life by the Christian, to whom he goes on to give what to us seems humdrum moral advice, telling him to be modest, affectionate, energetic, cheerful, persistent in prayer, hospitable, sympathetic, forgiving. Paul is not alone in this, in transposing the language of the sacrificial worship of the Temple to the living of the Christian life. The whole New Testament expresses the conviction, the growth of which we can trace in the Old, that the sacrifice that is *really* acceptable to God is a moral life of obedience to his will. This is the message of the prophets; the Temple sacrifices are only acceptable if they are the expression of a good life:

> With what shall I come before the Lord, and bow myself before God on high? Shall I come before him with burnt offerings, with calves a year old? Will the Lord be pleased with thousands of rams, with ten thousands of rivers of oil? Shall I give my first-born for my transgression, the fruit of my body for the sin of my soul? He has showed you, O man, what is good and what does the Lord require of you but to do justice, and to love kindness, and to walk humbly with your God? (Micah 6.6–8).

The burden of the Epistle to the Hebrews is that Jesus' sacrifice of himself, the sacrifice of a perfectly obedient life, sums up and supersedes the Temple sacrifices. The author quotes from Psalm 40 in the Septuagint version:

> Sacrifices and offerings thou hast not desired,
> but a body hast thou prepared for me;
> In burnt offerings and sin offerings thou hast taken no pleasure.
> Then I said, 'Lo, I have come to do thy will, O God' (Heb. 10.5–7).

And he continues:

> He abolishes the first in order to establish the second. And by that will we have been sanctified through the offering of the body of Jesus Christ once for all (Heb. 10.9 f.).

I Peter similarly interprets the levitical law of Holiness as demanding of Christians holiness of life.[3] For Christians, therefore, worship is bound up with the way they live – it has an ethical reference. In this respect Christianity is the heir of Israel, and the old and the new covenants are at one.

As the Jews reflected on their national origins and history, they came to recognize that the providence which had delivered, protected and established this small and downtrodden people, had shown himself a God of mercy and love. This is the same insight as Paul's, reflecting on his own

46

experience: 'God shows his love for us in that while we were yet sinners Christ died for us' (Rom. 5.8). And they came to recognize that the grateful response of worship that this God required was therefore also a moral one. Man is capable of reflecting the moral being of God. His response to God is worked out in what already in the Old Testament is unhesitatingly presented as the imitation of God in love of our neighbour;[4] what in the New becomes the imitation of Christ in whom the image of God in man is restored.[5] God's election of Israel called for a love from his people as unconditional as his own. Exodus 24 tells the story of the old covenant's sealing, as God and his people became one blood and shared a sacrificial meal.

The later story of the Old Testament is the story of the people's repeated faithlessness, and of God's reluctance to give them up. Israel's repudiation of the covenant was final, as the Fourth Gospel tells it, on Good Friday, when the Jews rejected Jesus with the cry, 'We have no king but Caesar' (John 19.15), so turning their backs on all their history. But Jesus, as the New Testament presents him, is also in his own person the last faithful Israelite, and in his life of complete integrity, and in his obedience even to death, perfectly fulfils the law. Underlying the accounts of the Last Supper,[6] with their deliberate echoes of Exodus 24, is the conviction that in Jesus the covenant is renewed. From him Israel is reborn to include potentially the whole human race.[7]

Thus the new covenant, like the old, has a moral basis. It is based, on the one hand, on God's loving initiative in creating the world, and, above all, in acting in the person of his Son to redeem and recreate it; on the other hand, it is based on the Christian people's unconditional self-offering in gratitude to God by a new life of service. So we can see, throughout the New Testament writings, how the proclamation of the gospel leads into an exposition of the Christian life, which is seen as a life of self-oblation in thanksgiving, a *eucharistic* life. Paul does this in his epistle to the Romans: in the first eleven chapters he sets out his gospel, what God has done; then he starts his ethical section with the famous 'therefore' at the beginning of chapter 12. This, or a similar conjunction, appears again and again in the New Testament, marking the same transition. The pattern of the preaching is always: 'God has acted, *therefore* repent!'

But there is this difference between the old and the new covenants. Whereas in the old, the unconditional demand for a moral response from man came more and more to be felt as the unbearable burden of the Law, pressing externally on his conscience, never capable of fulfilment, in the new the perfect response has been made once for all. Jesus was recognized as being himself the Gospel, the revelation of God's glory and of his love, the Word made flesh; Jesus was seen, too, as the perfectly obedient servant of God, completely identified with man. He is God's Word; he is also man's only perfect response to the Word.[8] 'Therefore he is the mediator of a new covenant, so that those who are called may receive the promised eternal inheritance' (Heb. 9.15).

The new covenant is unbreakable because it is sealed in the person of Jesus Christ, in whom, as a later theology said, a divine and a human nature are indissolubly united. And the Christian, who by his baptism partakes of the Spirit of Christ in the community which is his body, shares in this covenant and may call God his Father. On him the moral law does not press externally as a terrible and unanswerable demand; it is interior to him, written on his heart,[9] in whom Christ lives. This explains the fact that New Testament accounts of the Christian ethic are generally seen to be descriptive of Jesus as he was remembered in the tradition. Thus it has often been pointed out that in Paul's famous exposition of the spiritual gift of charity in I Corinthians 13 one may readily substitute for 'charity' the name of Jesus himself. It is only by virtue of his union with Christ that the Christian's 'reasonable worship', 'the offering of his body as a living sacrifice', is 'acceptable to God'. That is what the eucharist is for.

And that is why the basic shape of the eucharistic liturgy is so simple. It follows the pattern of the covenant: God's word evoking man's response.

The first half recalls in the reading of scripture and its exposition the wonderful works of God in Christ. In the primitive church this ministry of the word was not stereotyped; it continued as long as time permitted, for the duration of a meal perhaps, or, as with Paul at Troas, most of the night.[10] And when there was a baptism, which was itself a recapitulation, in the persons of the neophytes, of these self-same events, the readings might be omitted.[11]

The second half expresses the church's response to God, blessing and praising him. Again in early times neither the exact content nor the length of the great prayer, originally the *only* prayer in the liturgy, which voiced this thanksgiving, was fixed. But it would have followed the pattern of Jesus' own blessing of his Father over the cup on the night of his betrayal, a pattern which he had himself inherited from Jewish tradition, and had made his own in the light of the wonders of God that had attended his ministry.[12] The Jews blessed God in response to his love shown in creation and in the covenant of Exodus, and they looked forward to the re-establishing of David's kingdom. For the Christian, the heart of his praise is his thanksgiving for the new covenant, sealed in the blood of Jesus, and the promise of the kingdom already inaugurated by David's Son.

In the course of his blessing and praise of God the 'one who presides over the brethren',[13] following the example of Jesus, takes in his hands bread and a cup of wine, simple elements by means of which the assembled church signifies that its oblation of itself, in each of its members, in thanksgiving to the Father is only possible and acceptable by virtue of Jesus's own perfect self-offering and in union with him. The cup that is shared signifies the Christian's participation in the new covenant; the bread, broken and distributed, his membership of the one body, the body which Jesus had declared to be his own. Thus Paul wrote:

> When we bless 'the cup of blessing', is it not a means of sharing in the blood of Christ? When we break the bread, is it not a means of sharing in the body of Christ? Because there is one loaf, we, many as we are, are one body; for it is one loaf of which we all partake (I Cor. 10.16 f.).

The eating of a common meal, the sharing of the same food which is absorbed as the very substance of our body, has always been recognized, and is so still, as the effective symbol of the unity of a family, and of peace between men who have been strangers or at variance with one another. The presence of Christ in his Spirit, experienced and recognized by Christians in the celebration of the eucharist, was therefore most simply and naturally signified in the sharing of the one bread and the one cup. Thus the eucharistic reference in the accounts of Jesus' resurrection appearances, many of them in the context of meals – the walk to Emmaus, the Sunday gatherings in the upper room, the breakfast by the Sea of Galilee – is not difficult to discern.

The second half of the liturgy is preceded, either immediately or at some point before the service begins, by the people bringing gifts in kind or in money for the meal and for the poor; and these offerings of love include bread and wine, some of which will be used for the eucharist. In earlier times a Christian was called an 'offerer' rather than, as now, a 'communicant'. And as the giver may be discerned in the gift, the Christian may truly be said to have brought himself in thankful self-oblation to God. As St Augustine wrote: 'In that which the church offers its very self is offered'.[14] The *whole* second half of the liturgy, not just the so-called 'offertory', but the entire service from the offertory up to and including the communion, is an action of offering, for Christ takes the self-same elements that the people have brought and uses them to associate the people with himself in his uniquely acceptable sacrifice. And so communion is an integral part of the offering, not a receiving only but a giving, in which, caught up into the love of the Son for the Father, we, ourselves, are accepted in the Beloved. And, such is the mystery of love, being thus accepted, we become in our turn acceptable. Our lives become worthy of the adopted sons of God.

If this at all truly represents the original balance in Christian life and worship, we can see how that balance has at various times been disturbed, with the result that both doctrine and liturgy have become distorted. The two elements, God's word and man's response, are bound to remain, for they are integral to any Christianity, but their interrelation may be less satisfactorily expressed. A clear example is that whole medieval theology of the eucharist which regards the liturgy as essentially a drama. This has survived into modern times, and has contributed in no small measure to the obscuring of the meaning of the eucharistic signs and has therefore also largely lessened their force.

In the course of the Middle Ages the *whole* mass took on itself the meaning formerly occupied by the first half only, and came to be regarded as a dramatization of Calvary. This development can be traced to the failure of the Western church, where Latin was no longer or had never been commonly understood, to translate the readings of scripture into the vernacular, and to the decline of preaching in the liturgy, partly due to the growth of private masses. The lections, the offertory, the eucharistic prayer itself, and the ceremonies and private devotions that grew up round them, were thought to represent the saving Passion of Christ, and the liturgical commentaries of the period draw very unconvincing analogies to make this point. The result is that the response of the Christian community, which classically had been enshrined in the entire second half of the eucharist, was driven out of the liturgy altogether. At the mass, as it was now understood, a Christian could attend only as a spectator, and so his response became a *private* matter, the private worship of Christ in the Sacrament held up for his adoration, or very occasionally a *private* act of communion.

The view of the Protestant Reformers was profoundly affected by this shift of balance. They insist again on the ministry of the word, by restoring the reading of the Bible in the vulgar tongue, and by reinstating the sermon, but they remain thoroughly medieval in seeing the two ministries of word and sacrament as essentially *parallel*, the one setting out in words and the other in actions the saving work of God. And the response to both remains a private one. It is not surprising that the extremists practically abandon the sacraments altogether as superfluous, and retain and exalt the sermon alone in the regular Sunday worship of the congregation. Those who, more faithful to dominical institution, retain the eucharist, tend to see it (as the medieval catholic saw it) as a drama. They regard the 'breaking of bread' and the 'pouring of wine' (from a flagon into the chalice, a ceremony invented for the purpose) as the symbolic setting forth of Christ's death on the Cross, in order to arouse the individual faith of the believer. As these Reformers saw it (and this is still the belief and practice of many Christians), bread and wine are necessary for this action, and for communion, but no offering of them is intended or desired. The Christian's giving of himself is thus divorced from the elements, and the unity of his moral sacrifice with that of Christ is not significantly expressed in the liturgy.

For many centuries in the West, attendance at the eucharist has been a matter only of public duty or of private devotion. Over the last decades, for multitudes of Christians, it has rapidly become again the very centre of their consciousness of being the church, the sign of the fulfilment of their humanity, both individually and socially. And this promises to bring to new life many aspects of the Christian tradition that have long been in the theological lumber-room of the historical scholar, and not least the doctrine of the Trinity. For a profounder grasp of the theology of the eucharist reveals the trinitarian pattern of God's self-revelation and likewise the trinitarian pattern of man's response. Since the long and painful controversies of the fourth and fifth centuries, Christians have been taught to pray, for safety's sake, 'Glory be to the Father, *and* to the Son, *and* to the Holy Ghost'; and thus a whole dynamic theology of prepositions (*through* the Son, *in* the Spirit) has been neglected, and Christian life and worship has suffered as a consequence. For when the church again knows itself in the Spirit to be worshipping the Father in union with and through the mediation of Christ, then a whole range of images is revived; as can be seen today in the sudden flowering of new church architecture, after centuries of pastiche.

Thus at the liturgy the presence of Christ among his people is symbolized in two ways, to both of which the building and the action must attend, and each focal to one part of the service. In the first half, as God's revelation in Jesus Christ is recalled, his presence is seen in the Bible from which the lections are read. That is why Christians have stood for the gospel, and surrounded it with all the respect at their command. Christ's presence in the second half of the liturgy is symbolized by the altar, which Christians reverence. The altar is Jacob's stone, Beth-el, the house of God and gate of heaven, where stands the ladder on which angels ascend and descend. Jesus is himself that ladder.[15] And the altar is the table where God's people share the 'Bread of Heaven in Christ Jesus',[16] a foretaste of the banquet of the kingdom.[17]

The Bible and the table, bread and wine. The simplicity of the early liturgy was well characterized by Dom Gregory Dix, when he wrote of the early Christian that

what brought him to the eucharist week by week, despite all dangers and inconveniences, was no thrill provoked by the service itself, which was bare and unimpressive to the point of dullness, and would soon lose any attraction of novelty.[18]

For it is the presence of Christ in the liturgy which constitutes the Christian mystery; and this is not a mystery before which men bow in superstitious dread, but in which

53

they participate by hearing gladly the word of God and by giving themselves in his service.

It is true that such a service will find a man out if his life is not permeated by the gospel, but for this no elaborate ceremony, no conscious attempt to rouse the emotions, no dim religious light can substitute. The Christian mystery is a mystery *revealed*, the hidden purpose of God disclosed in the fullness of time in Jesus Christ and made known through the church.[19] And of this church the beating heart is the eucharist, its daily breathing in and breathing out, whereby the Holy Spirit gives it life; now drawing into itself man's whole response of thanksgiving, bringing him as an oblation in Christ before God, now sending him out into and through the world that it may be renewed. So, in the church, man finds himself again in his true nature, *homo eucharisticus*.

NOTES

1. Cf. p. 40.

2. Cf. I Cor. 11.26; Heb. 10.25.

3. Cf. I Peter 1.16.

4. Cf. e.g. Ex. 22.21; 23.9; Lev. 19.34; Deut. 10.19.

5. Cf. e.g. Matt. 5.44 f., 48; John 13.34; Eph. 4.32–5.2; I John 3.16; 4.10 f., 19.

6. Mark 14.22–5; Matt. 26.26–9; Luke 22.17–19; I Cor. 11.23–6.

7. In John 19.34 the waters of baptism and the wine of the eucharist are clearly referred to; cf. also I Cor. 15.45 ff.

8. Cf. Mark 1.1; John 1.14; Phil. 2.5–8; Heb. 1.2 f.; 2.9–11; 4.15; I John 4.7–9.

9. Cf. Jer. 31.31–34.

10. Cf. Acts 20.7 ff.

11. Cf. Justin Martyr, *First Apology*, 65–7.

12. Cf. J.-P. Audet, 'Literary Forms and Contents of a Normal *eucharistia* in the First Century', in *Studia Evangelica* (1959), pp. 643 ff.

13. Justin Martyr, *op. cit.*, 65.

14. Augustine, *The City of God*, 10.6.

15. Cf. Gen. 28.11–17; John 1.51.

16. Hippolytus, *op. cit.*, 23.

17. Cf. Matt. 22.1–14; Luke 22.30.

18. G. Dix, *The Shape of the Liturgy* (London: Dacre Press, 1945). p. 153.

19. Cf. Eph. 3.7 ff.; also Mark 4.11; Rom. 16.25f; I Cor. 2.7; Eph. 1.9; 6.19; Col. 1.26; I Tim. 3.16.

5 The Assembly

The church is most visibly itself at the eucharistic assembly, so much so that in the New Testament we can see the church defined in terms of the eucharist. The church is called *ecclesia*, which means simply the 'assembly'; and *Corpus Christi*, the body of Christ, has from New Testament times to the present day been used both to signify the loaf of the eucharist and as a collective noun for the multitude of Christ's disciples. Already in the Old Testament the 'assembly', meeting together in one place, is thought of as fundamental to Israel, as is witnessed by the desire to gather together all adult Jews in Jerusalem for the great festivals, a principle extended and necessarily mitigated by regarding the synagogue as a reflection of the Temple. Again, both Jewish and Christian eschatology has usually thought of the end of the world in terms of a general assize.[1] Thus while the Hebrew word *qāhāl*, variously translated *ecclesia*, assembly, or church, came in fact to designate the people only theoretically assembled, in God's sight as it were, the basic idea of actual meeting was never totally abandoned. And it is this aspect that takes on new life and meaning in the church, to which, as to the idealized Israel of old, God has promised his presence and guidance night and day.[2] It was for this reason, as Dom Gregory Dix pointed out so forcefully, that the early Christians, even in virtual certainty of arrest, clung to the eucharistic *assembly* (not just to communion, which they often in any case had privately at home from the reserved sacrament) as to a life-line, for without it they did not constitute the church of Jesus Christ:

55

It was to secure the fullness of this corporate action that a presbyter *and a deacon* had to be smuggled somehow into the imperial prisons, there to celebrate their last eucharist for the confessors awaiting execution; and Cyprian takes it as a matter of course that this must be arranged. . . . To secure this was always the first thought of Christians in time of threatened persecution. 'But how shall we meet, you ask, how shall we celebrate the Lord's solemnities? . . . If you cannot meet by day, there is always the night,' says Tertullian, bracing the fearful to stay and meet the coming storm. Even when a church had been scattered by long persecution, the duty was never forgotten. 'At first they drove us out and . . . we kept our festival even then, pursued and put to death by all, and every single spot where we were afflicted became for us a place of assembly for the feast – field, desert, ship, inn, prison,' writes Denys, bishop of Alexandria, of one terrible Easter day *c.* AD 250, when a raging civil war, famine and pestilence were added to the woes of his persecuted church.[3]

We can see therefore how, as the eucharist came less and less to be the sharing together of the common loaf, the image of the church as Christ's body becomes a mere theological fiction. The sense of Christ's presence becomes localized, to be worshipped from afar, the preserve of the clergy who alone communicate regularly; and the church as a whole ceases to think of itself as a sign of the kingdom.

The critical point was reached, as Father J.-P. Audet has argued,[4] when what he calls the *communauté de base*, the basic group of the church's life, ceased to be modelled on the prototype of the 'household' and adopted the altogether different model of the 'crowd', a transition that is typified in architecture by the change from the house-church to the basilica, from a private to a public building. Whereas at the outset the group was of a size that corresponded to the conditions demanded by the ministries of the word and of the sacraments, if these were to be effective, now on the contrary these ministries had to be adapted to groups whose size was continually growing, and this was less and less successful. Thus what had been essentially family instruction[5] became the public rhetoric of preaching, and the eloquent sacramental signs of communal life were, as we have seen, obscured. And here Father Audet makes a telling comparison:

> If you invite a small number of relations or friends to your house, you will ask them to sit down at your table and you will yourself serve them with the best food that you have. If you invite twenty-five people, whom you know in very different ways, I suppose you would provide a cold buffet. If fifty people came, to whom you are connected even more variously, you would alter the time of the occasion and would invite them, I should think, to a garden-party, and would arrange for refreshments. If two hundred people are invited, you might still give them a meal, but you would put the matter into the hands of professional caterers. As far as you are concerned, you would content yourself with greeting personally only some of your guests, and you would make a little speech of welcome to the assembled company. . . . What I want to underline is that numbers necessarily change the form and the content of human relationships. This is a law which we cannot avoid, and least of all perhaps in the delicate ministry of word and sacrament.

It is from this period that we can trace that view of the church which regards its structures, its unity, and the authority exercised within it, primarily in terms of centralized power, whether in terms of a papal Roman Empire whose provinces were governed in the name of a spiritual Caesar by his pro-consuls, the bishops; or of Protestant nations, in which the godly prince was the effective governor, and every clergyman a representative of the establishment. Today that view survives in the assumption that the churches are primarily religious organizations in need of central government and bureaucracy, as is exemplified in all the great denominations of the West.

Indeed the existence of denominational 'churches' is largely responsible for the persistence of this state of affairs. In contrast with the 'horizontal' association in sacramental charity of local churches (which may indeed be grouped, as is still the case in the East, in provinces, nations, and international patriarchates) in denominations local churches are, so to speak, 'vertically' connected, so that they may call on support from above to maintain a particular theological line against rival churches in the same locality. Such rivalries readily harden when factors, such as social class, are added to, and then often supersede, theological controversy. In these circumstances the local churches' prime concern soon becomes the maintenance of their own life, and evangelism, if it is practised at all, is thought of as recruiting for membership.

Meanwhile the superstructure that grows up to support, defend, and promote the local church, takes on a life of its own, and soon comes to regard the local churches as 'branches' of an organization of which it is the all-wise management, though usually it is enlightened enough to consult the local members from time to time.

It is important to be precise at this point. Churches have always looked to other churches beyond their immediate neighbourhood for help and inspiration; the New Testament provides ample evidence of this. Apostolic preaching and teaching; the itinerant prophets; the hospitality of Christians to each other, which was such a feature of the early churches' life; the collection made by Paul among the Gentiles for the church in Jerusalem; and, not least, ceaseless prayer for one another; all these bound them together. The promotion and preservation of unity in these and other respects needed then, as they always will, patient labour and watchfulness; and John Knox describes the church's history in the first century of its life partly as an 'ecumenical movement'.[6] So today it is of course reasonable that churches should make use of common resources and should employ people to administer them, in Christian literature and education for example.

What is in question is the development of distinctive sub-cultures within Christianity (Catholic*ism*, Anglican*ism*, Method*ism*, Presbyterian*ism*, etc.), for these effectively hinder the local church from being sufficiently sensitive to the needs of the world in which it is set, to its social patterns and cultural forms. And it is inevitably the denominational superstructures that keep these sub-cultures in being.

The Lutheran minister in industrial Germany in his

sixteenth-century ruff; the Anglican priest in Africa dressed in surplice, hood, and scarf; the Catholic friar in the United States in his expensively tailored habit – these are still familiar figures, and speak respectively of the Augsburg Confession, the XXXIX Articles, and the Council of Trent. The overseas missions in particular were often in large measure a form of cultural colonialism, a fact to which the gothic and baroque churches, and the liturgies and music of their congregations, left behind by the receding tide of European imperial power, bear eloquent testimony. And when to this is added the long retention of executive leadership and financial control by Europeans, the superficial impact of Christianity in Asia and Africa is not difficult to understand. And still this is to say nothing of the much profounder assumption that only European philosophical and mythological categories are adequate to the expression of Christian belief – as when St Francis Xavier in the sixteenth-century told his Japanese listeners that their ancestors were in hell: to which they very properly replied, that in that case they were perfectly content to go there themselves.

It was this attitude which Wilkie Collins satirized a century ago in *The Moonstone* in his portrait of Miss Drusilla Clack, a Christian lady of the tract-distributing variety. At one point she pauses to define what she means by a true Christian and his mission:

Once self-supported by conscience, once embarked on a career of manifest usefulness, the true Christian never yields. Neither public nor private influence produce the slightest effect on us, when we have once got our mission. . . . riots may be the consequence of a mission; wars may be the consequence of a mission; we go on with our work, irrespective of every human consideration which moves the world outside us. We are above reason; we are beyond ridicule; we see with nobody's eyes, we hear with nobody's ears, we feel with nobody's hearts, but our own. Glorious, glorious privilege! And how is it earned? Ah, my friends, you may spare yourselves the useless enquiry! We are the only people who can earn it – for we are the only people who are always right.[7]

Once we have got our mission . . . above reason, insensitive to the world, always right – if this is a caricature it nevertheless has the devastating likeness of caricature, the emphasis on distinctive features that makes us understand why many have rejected Christianity not so much for being unworldly as for being inhuman. For the significance of Wilkie Collins' satire is that behind it lies a *moral* protest. It is a protest against Christianity in the name of humanity, of which the great nineteenth- and early twentieth-century poets and novelists were the prophets. It is this protest, much more than any metaphysical difficulty, which has put Christianity out of court for the greater number of educated men and women today, who are disposed to think that they cannot be Christians and also reasonable, and moved by worldly considerations, and sometimes wrong. Being a Christian, they feel, involves a certain closing of the mind, a cutting through the complexities of social and personal relationships, a narrowing of their manhood and womanhood. Perhaps the most disturbing aspect of Christian theology in general in the last centuries has been its lack of humility, and it must seem now that the confidence of much dogmatic and moral theology in speaking of God and of God's will for man has rested less on the perception of faith than on an increasing blindness and deafness towards the contemporary realities of God's world.

For we must recognize that there seems always to have been a strain in Christianity which has undervalued the doctrine of creation, which has opposed grace to nature. This is the Christianity that interpreted *extra ecclesiam nulla salus*, 'no salvation outside the church', in the strict sense of condemning as the *massa damnata* all those not safe in the visible ark of the church, and was confident that it knew exactly where to draw the church's boundaries. It is in this tradition that many, though certainly not all, the Puritans, both Catholic and Protestant, stood; and which at repeated intervals in the church's history has been carried to extremes by those exclusive sects, which cannot accept that the church should be made up of sinners, of men and women whose salvation in Christ has still to be worked out in the course of their lives.

Against such a faith, which owes more to the Pharisees than to Jesus, every moral protest is justified; for it is manifest that it is this strain in Christianity which has always come to the fore when the opportunity of power and influence has been presented. And it is far from dead. We no longer have the stake; economic sanctions against nonconforming tenants are past; the interfering Miss Clack is a rarity. But there are still Christians ready to resort to the psychological pressures of the advertiser, ready to play on men's anxieties and fears, ready to force doors at which Christ himself is content to knock.

Against this whole view the reassertion of the sacramental character of the church stands in the sharpest possible contrast. And nowhere has this reassertion been clearer or more vigorous than in the Constitution on the church, *De Ecclesia*, of the Second Vatican Council, a council that began its deliberations with a document on the liturgy. *De Ecclesia* is inevitably a composite document and propounds in some of its chapters an uncompromisingly authoritarian view of the church, particularly in respect of the papacy. But these passages read like the tired, and sometimes shrill, protestations of men who feel their positions threatened.

The main emphasis of the Constitution is quite other. Here the principle of unity in the church is discerned to be the Holy Spirit, and the bonds between the members of the body are the bonds of that charity which is his work (7).[8] The great biblical images of the church recur again and again, notably that of the people of God. Into that people all men are called, to the 'dignity and freedom of God's sons', to the 'new law of a love like the love that Christ has shown to us', to the 'goal of God's kingdom' (9). The Constitution forswears all double standards and insists that all men without distinction 'are called to the fullness of the Christian life and the perfection of charity', and this involves the

61

search for a 'more humane way of life on earth' (40) and the struggle for social justice (36); and it is in this spirit that it warns against the deceptive affluence of our society (42).

De Ecclesia is careful to distinguish the church and the kingdom of God. Its 'mission is to announce the kingdom of Christ and of God, and to inaugurate it among all nations, for it is the seed and the beginning of this kingdom on earth' (5). The church is repeatedly spoken of as 'being on pilgrimage' (6). 'The church is made up of sinners, and so it is at the same time holy and always in need of purification, as it constantly seeks renewal in penitence' (8). This remarkable statement is reminiscent of Hans Küng's protest in his book *The Council and Reunion*, written before the Council, against that tendency in the past which idealized the church and thought of it as somehow existing independently of the sinful men of whom it is composed.[9]

This approach led the Council, for the first time in a Roman Catholic document, to see membership of the church as in some sense extended beyond those in visible communion with the Roman See. All the baptized are unreservedly called Christians and their profession of many elements of Catholic faith and practice is acknowledged. More important still is the recognition, implied in speaking of these Christians as possessing churches or ecclesial communities, that Christian belief is inseparable from membership in the Christian fellowship (15). Christians not in communion with Rome are no longer stigmatized as individual wanderers in the twilight. It is strange to recall that less than eighty years ago Cardinal Vaughan believed that the revival of sacramental practice in the Church of England was the work of the devil, designed to prevent men from entering the true fold. The Constitution, on the contrary, says of non-Catholics that 'they too possess a real unity in the Holy Spirit, for in them also his sanctifying power produces his gifts and graces, and in his strength some of them have even shed their blood. Thus the Spirit is prompting in all Christ's disciples both the desire and action to bring about unity and peace, according to Christ's will' (15).

De Ecclesia further speaks positively of the relationship with the church of those who are not Christians: the Jews, the Moslems, and all seekers after God. They too are related to the people of God and included in the promise of salvation (16). More, the readiness of the church to accept all that is good in human life and culture is underlined, and 'no seed of good in the hearts and minds of men is lost, but is healed, raised, and fulfilled to God's glory' (16, 17).

But the most telling words of the whole document come in the very first paragraph. 'The church is, in Christ, the sacrament, that is the sign and the means, of the unity of all men with God and with one another.'

It is this idea that the Jesuit theologian Karl Rahner develops in speaking about the church of the future.[10] He foresees the time when men will

> not be Christians by custom or tradition, through institutions and history, or because of the homogeneity of a social milieu and public opinion, but, apart from the influence of a family or small group, only because of their own act of faith.

There will no longer be nations 'which put a Christian stamp on men prior to any personal decision'. Christians will be a minority, probably a smaller minority than now, dispersed throughout the world. Yet they will not regard themselves as the saved among the great *massa damnata*, but as the sign of the salvation of the whole world:

> The church is not the society of those who alone are saved, but the sign of the salvation of those who, as far as its historical and social structure is concerned, do not belong to it. By their profession of faith, their worship and life, the human beings in the church form as it were the one expression in which the hidden grace promised and offered to the whole world emerges from the abysses of the human soul into the domain of history and society. This grace of the world has an inner dynamic tendency to assume tangible historical form in the church. Grace can be present and operative to an immeasurable extent in the world and its history without everywhere in the course of history finding tangible social expression in the Church. The Christian will not call men's kindness, love, fidelity to conscience,

'natural' virtues, which are only really found in the abstract. He will think that the grace of Christ is at work even in those who have never expressly invoked it. In preaching Christianity to 'non-Christians', therefore, the future Christian will not so much start with the idea that he is aiming at turning them into something they are not, as trying to bring them to their true selves.

Karl Rahner is clear that revelation cannot simply be identified with the 'historical, explicit, verbally formulated revelation' of the Old and New Testaments, 'where it has its pure historical manifestation and eschatological finality', 'any more than the conferring of grace is identical with the sacramental conferring of grace'. And he faces an obvious difficulty:

Does this overlook the sin, error, darkness, and danger of eternal perdition in the world? No, it is not the case that such optimism of faith comes easily to modern men. . . . Men were probably never so little convinced of their own goodness, so aware of their fragility, so miserably conscious of their vulnerability, the possibility and probability that their holiest idealism may be unmasked as fear, as a vital need of security, cowardice, lack of vitality. Man experiences his finiteness, his poverty, his vulnerability, his utter opennness to question. If despite all this he is obedient to God's word and thinks what is noble and holy of men, believes (it is not easy) that he is a child of God, loved by God and worthy of an eternal life which is already operative and growing within him, he will not be haughty and proud, will not regard what is promised as being his inalienable right.

Will this mean less missionary zeal?

On the contrary it is easier and less restrictive to be able to say to to someone, 'Become what you are', than, 'Destroy what you were until now'.

This is the gospel of the Prologue of John, where, making use of the Stoic concept of the *Logos*, John speaks of the Word as the light that lightens everyman (John 1.9), made flesh in him who in his exaltation will draw all men to himself (John 12.32) and 'gather into one the children of God who are scattered abroad' (John 11.52); and it is with the *Logos* in mind, who was thought of as the shepherd of the universe, that he represents Jesus saying, 'And I have other sheep that are not of this fold; I must bring them also, and they will heed my voice. So there shall be one flock and one shepherd' (John 10.16). Earlier already, Paul had used another Stoic concept, that of the body of humanity, to illuminate his doctrine of the church.[11]

This is the gospel preached by Paul at Athens in which he quotes the Greek poets[12]; the Christianity which begins with the belief that God has not left himself without witness in a world that is his by virtue of his creating and sustaining it;[13] and, acknowledging that God has of old spoken by the prophets, sees in the Son the heir of all things through whom the world was created.[14] This is the Christianity of the Fathers, who number the Old Testament heroes among the saints,[15] and Virgil among the prophets; which traces Jesus' ancestry to Adam[16] and sees in the church the nucleus of the new humanity, the world in the process of becoming what from the beginning it was intended to be. Such a faith can adopt as its own the poet Terence's motto, 'Nothing that is human is foreign to me.'[17]

NOTES

1. Cf. Matt. 25.31 f.
2. Cf. e.g. Ex. 13.21 f.; I Kings 7.15, 21; 8.10 f.; Matt. 18.20; 28.20; John 2.19–21; 14.3–6, 26; Rev. 21.3, 22; and the tradition of the Lord's command at the institution of the eucharist, 'Do this in remembrance of me' (I Cor. 11.24f).
3. G. Dix, *op. cit.*, pp. 152 f.
4. J.–P. Audet, *Mariage et Célibat dans le service pastoral de l'Église* (Paris, 1967), summarized in *Maintenant* No. 71, November 1967, pp. 334–7.
5. Acts 20.20; I Thess. 2.11 f.
6. J. Knox, *The Early Church and the Coming Great Church* (New York: Abingdon Press, 1955, and London: Epworth, 1957), p. 17. This subject will be treated more fully in Chapters 8 and 9.
7. Wilkie Collins, *The Moonstone* (Everyman's Library), p. 209.
8. The Second Vatican Council, *Dogmatic Constitution on the Church.* The English version most readily available is published by the Catholic Truth Society, 1965. I have taken the liberty of amending this translation in a number of places. References in parentheses are to paragraphs.

9. H. Küng, *The Council and Reunion* (London: Sheed & Ward, 1961) pp. 34 ff.; cf. also his new book, *The Church* (New York: Herder and Herder, and London: Burns & Oates, 1968), pp. 319 ff.

10. Cf. *Herder Correspondence*, July 1965.

11. Cf. e.g. I Cor. 12.12–27.

12. Acts, 17.28.

13. Acts 14.17.

14. Heb. 1.1 f.; cf. John 1.3.

15. The calendars of the Eastern Churches still do this.

16. Luke 3.23–38.

17. '*Homo sum; humani nil a me alienum puto*', Terence (*c.* 190–159 BC) *Heauton Timorumenos*, I. i. 25.

66

6 Shapes

For more than fifteen hundred years the church has dominated European culture. Christianity has shaped men's ideas and their way of life so decisively that it is difficult for us to stand outside our metaphysical, moral and aesthetic traditions, and to evaluate them. Yet there is an urgent need to do just this, for the church's uncertainties can only be resolved as Christians learn to understand better the necessary relationships and mutual influence of their faith with the society to which they speak. For if the church has largely formed the pattern of our world, the world in its turn has determined the shape of the church and the way in which Christian belief is formulated. This point is well made by Leslie Paul near the beginning of his study of the clergy of the Church of England. It is right, he says, to speak of the church transcending the particular times and cultures of men; nevertheless it is also and always

a social institution affected by and in its turn affecting the social patterns within which it operates. More, the more successful it is as spiritual mentor of its congregation the more important it becomes as a social influence. Perhaps the corollary is also true. The more successful it is as a social influence, the more it has to struggle to prevent its spiritual life from being subjected to society, or made the instrument of society; the more it must labour self-critically to keep its sources pure. Equally, the more it fails in its religious tasks, the feebler its social impact becomes. Within the terms of such an understanding it is sensible, and even obligatory, to look at the church first as an earthly institution, asking the questions one would ask of other institutions, and then as a social institution rooted in a particular society at a particular time, seeking to change its behaviour patterns, but also limited and conditioned by them.[1]

The church has no predetermined institutional pattern. Its own structures follow the structures of the society in which it takes root. We tend to forget that this is precisely what happened in the great evangelistic periods of the first thousand years of the Christian history, when the church adapted itself to the world it found. Thus in Southern Europe, where Christianity came to countries already full of little towns, a diocese to this day consists of a town and its surrounding country district, each with its own bishop; whereas in the uncivilized North dioceses are few and far between, with bishops who bravely sally forth from their Roman encampments, as the names of many English dioceses still testify.

It was the success of the church in adapting itself to the varied human societies into which it came that led those same societies, when the Empire was disintegrating, to turn to the church for the preservation of that overarching frame of reference which Roman rule had ensured. And so, as we saw, the church came to underpin the world of men, and the values of the world corrupted it. Its very success was its downfall, for, as it came to confuse the ordering of existence here and now under the rule of the church with the kingdom of God, it sacralized the world and lost its own perspective. It could no longer change the world, indeed it became the most potent force *resisting* change.

Yet this Christendom was precariously balanced. Reading between the lines of its history (largely of course clerically written) we can discern what today might be called an 'anti-Christendom' underneath; on the one hand an earthy, humorous, anti-clerical protest, that sometimes also becomes nihilistic, and, on the other, an attempt, as with the Franciscan movement, or with Wycliffe and Huss, to return to a more authentic Christian stance in and to the world. Christendom survived the Reformation because the principle of *cuius regio, eius religio* effectively left the church allied with the Christian prince in the rule of each nation, whatever combination of the 'old' and the 'new' religion it professed. But when under the continued secularizing impact of new world discoveries, the spread of literacy, and the growth of the natural sciences, this unified world broke up, the church had become so identified with that particular order that it was left almost helplessly staring at the pieces.

Not that the attempt to put them together again has not been made. In the years before the second world war, both in England and on the continent, some of the best Christian minds devoted themselves to this end. The 'Christendom' group, significantly so called, was long the centre of some of the best thinking about the relation of Christianity to contemporary society, its social problems as well as its art, theatre and literature. And in France the 'neo-Thomist' movement in Christian philosophy, associated with the name of Jacques Maritain, was inspired by similar motives.

This same nostalgia shows itself in the appeals and lamentations of some church leaders, pathetically recalling the modern world to religious and moral standards of a past age. The church, so represented, is looking *backwards*, attempting vainly to persuade men of a gospel that is 'bad news' for them, but, unfortunately, true. This perspective apparently justifies the continued attempt of the church to cling to what power it can for the good of society, whether men like it or not. This fight for power may be overt, as in the campaign to prevent the legalizing of divorce in Italy, or politically more subtle, in the deploying of pressure groups at the sensitive points of a society where decisions are made.

In the life of the church generally the same preoccupation may be detected behind a frequently expressed concern for the preservation and promotion of so-called 'organic' groups and communities – in particular the family in its present form. The fact that the church is still at its most effective in villages and market towns which have retained an older and therefore more readily intelligible social structure, has generally led it to attempt to recreate that structure in quite different situations, in an industrial area, for example, or in suburbia. In new areas the first task of the church is seen to be the creation of a sense of community, the forging of links between people at a natural level, which the atomizing of our society have broken. And there are those who, doubting the possibility of this, are pessimistic of the church's finding a way to live in such a world. The result of this policy is in effect the making of artificial 'villages' round the parish church. Whether the population of the geographical parish is three thousand or twenty thousand, the number of people associated with the church in any way will be at the most about five hundred – people who know all about one another, like and loathe one another, accept an unspoken hierarchy among themselves, and love above all their harvest festival. Such churches betray their likeness to 'village' communities in other aspects of their group behaviour. They lose the great majority of their young people, although these were nurtured with immense pains when they were children, because the size of the community limits the number of useful roles open to the young when they grow up. They are suspicious of strangers, who at first sight represent a threat to the settled ways of the place. And they put an immense pressure to conform on their members. The local church frequently becomes a right-thinking, right-behaving social group. In effect, if not in intention, this group is exclusive and makes great psychological demands on those it invites to belong. This is one reason why the poor, the West Indian immigrant population in England for example, which was generally and cheerfully church-going at home, see the church as yet one more unanswerable demand that an affluent society makes on them, and to which, as to the lures of other self-interested bodies, they have to develop a sales-resistance. Society imprisons them as it is; the church threatens to close the sky over them as well.

For, ironically, in the aftermath of Christendom, the roles of church and world have been reversed. The church that formerly ruled is now dethroned, not to be rejected altogether and despised, but to be used for the world's own ends. This is the penalty it has paid for abandoning its former perspective, for letting Christians forget that 'their existence is on earth, but their citizenship in heaven'.[2]

And this raises doubts about an image of the church, much favoured today – the 'servant' church; an image that points the contrast with the so-called 'triumphalist' church in the centuries of its power. It is inspired by Jesus' reported words in Mark 10.42–5, telling his disciples that he who would be great among them must become their servant; but it often conceals a readiness to identify the church with the world's concerns as uncritical as any in the previous era. And it can mask the old craving for power, the power, below stairs now, of the servant who makes himself indispensable and has his master's ear, the power of the useful humanitarian agency that tidies up, keeps the house clean, and salves the world's conscience.

Once again one of the most telling protests against this continuing worldliness of the church comes in a novel. Angus Wilson's *Late Call* is set in the bright, planned society of a new town. At one moment he sees this society, in all its absurdity, reflected in the Easter morning service at the church in the town centre.

> Mrs Marchant, the vicar's wife, a dowdy cheerful-looking woman, was in the atrium among the unvarnished wooden tables and book racks all stacked up with pamphlets each with a clever eye-catching photograph on its cover. 'I'm so terribly sorry,' she said to everyone, 'Kenneth's slipped a disc. And we had to take what the archdeacon could send us at the last moment.'

So instead of a sermon comparable to the excellent one the previous Easter on the 'eleven-plus', the go-ahead new town church had had to suffer what Harold Calvert, the local headmaster, afterwards summed up as 'vicious nonsense'. 'I suppose few more barbaric doctrines have disgraced humanity than all this rubbish about Grace . . . .' 'No,' the old priest had said to a congregation, murmuring with disappointment and embarrassment, 'not all the charity, the social work as they call it now, can save your soul alive if there's no soul left to save. . . .'[3]

Of such a congregation, and many like it, Charles Davis has written:

Christian truth disturbs and arouses opposition; the average church congregation provides social adjustment into the world, the values and the social class of the neighbourhood. For that reason, the present denominations frequently function as anti-Christian institutions. By this I mean that their political, social and cultural impact reinforces values and activities that contradict Christian teaching and values. I do not have in mind here simply the glaring instances where the Christian churches have supported, and still do support, iniquitous political and social orders. But there are the more hidden ways in which the effect of existing denominational institutions is anti-Christian. In *The Noise of Solemn Assemblies*, Peter Berger shows how the social function of the Protestant churches in the United States is to provide a symbolic integration of the present values of American society, values such as success through competitive struggle, activism, and so on, which are not those of Christ. The churches are emphatically reinforcing social and political values alien to Christianity.[4]

Christianity has become one among many religions, each upholding their particular culture. And in the case of Christianity this may be a culture whose values are far removed from those of the gospel.

The shape the church is left with, therefore, is partly that of the world as it once was, and partly that assumed under the pressure of denominational organization and rivalry. Such a shape has been mistaken as predetermined and divinely guaranteed, only because, as the world changed much and the church hardly at all, the shape it retained became peculiarly its own. To believe this to be immutable merely serves to legitimize a nostalgia for a vanished age and the reluctance to relinquish present positions comfortably secured.

And it inhibits the possibility of adaptation to new circumstances. The clearest evidence of this is the failure of the church to evangelize the emergent working class from the time of the urbanization of England, because its presuppositions and the rigidity of its machinery prevented it deploying its forces. In East London in the early eighteenth century, for example, the Church of England could think only in terms of building magnificent baroque temples, whose vast expense meant that finally only twelve were built, though the Acts of Parliament required for the purpose had envisaged fifty. In this respect the Nonconformists, still at a relatively flexible stage of their development, had a much better record.[5]

If, therefore, today we ask whether the church has a future other than as a society existing mainly for its own sake, and unconsciously dominated by the values of its social context, the answer will depend on how far Christians are prepared to see that the present shape of the church effectively withdraws them from concern with the life, the work, and the problems of their neighbours. For even much Christian reformist energy is then devoted to purely ecclesiastical ends. It is only if the church's structures are contemporary that Christian thinking about the needs of men, as they are related to one another in the world, is not clouded by preoccupations about the best use of inherited ecclesiastical institutions. For there are no single and simple answers. Different parts of the world, indeed different parts of the same country, are in different stages of development, and this means that while in some places traditional answers may still be valid, in many others quite new approaches are called for.

The church's parochial system came into being because the countries of Europe at the time were countries of villages. England is still assumed to be so; when banns of marriage are called in church, it is taken for granted that the people concerned are well known to everybody. The rural deaneries in their turn corresponded (and sometimes still do) with the hundreds. Today's centres of population are infinitely more complex, and need to be looked at from a number of different perspectives. On the one hand there are the more or less readily definable areas in which living, working, schooling, marketing, and entertainment draw the boundaries of a locality. Local government boundaries and responsibilities are presently under review because they are seen to be strangling the possibilities of social and economic growth. *Mutatis mutandis* the church stands in the same necessity. On the other hand, there are recognizable lines of human relationships within and beyond these areas, in family and friendship ties, in work, and in socially concerned and active groups. A family that lives in a suburban house or a block of flats may be linked in very various ways with people nearby or at a distance, relations, colleagues at work, and others who share common interests. An urban life also has patterns, though much more complicated and shifting ones than a village. But, as Harvey Cox has said, 'urban anonymity need not be heartless. Village sociability can mask a murderous hostility.'[6] Mobility and anonymity have helped men to break social and economic barriers, have meant infinitely greater possibilities of choice in their lives, of friends, of where they live, of what talents they wish to develop both for work and for leisure. That there is a dark side to this has already been emphasized, but, while it is certainly and particularly the church's vocation to care for the lonely and neglected in modern society, as in any other, this care can only come from Christians in a church which is consonant with the variety and complexity of that society.

Reflecting on mid-nineteenth-century England, John Henry Newman boldly protested against the restoration of the Roman Catholic hierarchy in 1851:

We want seminaries far more than sees. We want education, view, combination, organization.

The society of his day seemed to call for a

great organization going round the towns, giving lectures or making speeches . . . starting a paper, a review, etc.[7]

Such open-mindedness is little rarer today than it was over a century ago. The church has hardly begun to take seriously the need to modify its institutions. And when experiments are undertaken, the results are rarely evaluated or the lessons learnt consistently carried through. It is much commoner, when pioneers move on and individual enthusiasm flags, for the old ways to reassert themselves. For even where there is a desire for change, the fact that the church conceives of itself in terms of a centrally governed organization, or rather as a set of such organizations, makes the implementation of changes extremely slow, and often too late. If a central representative body has to collect information from widely diverse situations, consider it, and make recommendations for the implementation of a general policy, which in the circumstances is bound to be a compromise, it is not surprising that little that is effective is done. Central government and central bureaucracy may preserve a semblance of unity of purpose, but this means again and again that the few patches where new blades of grass are actually springing up are liable to be stamped on for letting spring come too soon.

The possibility of the church reforming itself from the centre is remote, though in all the denominations an official liberalizing of old rules and the authorizing of experimentation in worship and ministry is in hand. This has generally been agreed despite the bitterly fought opposition of a conservative minority, which rightly perceives that the old order is a unity, and that, once this unity is broken in one particular, the whole edifice is likely to fall. If, for example, one considers the immense patience with which over nine hundred years since the days of Hildebrand, Gregory VII, the papal government of the Roman church has been built up, it is not difficult to sympathize with those who tremble to see the whole system being dismantled with such enthusiasm almost overnight. And before long it is the original reformers who are desperately calling for restraint, for there is no conservatism more anxious than that of the liberal overtaken by revolution. Like the sorcerer's apprentice he is liable to turn back to the old certainties: only in his case there is no sorcerer to restore matters as they were before.

There is a 'panic feeling that things have got out of control'.[8] Whereas this is most obvious in Roman Catholicism, as a direct result of the calling of the Second Vatican Council, other denominations manifest similar anxieties, though being mostly smaller, more tolerant of variation, or institutionally more diverse than Rome, the strains are less apparent to an outside observer. Here, paradoxically, the Church of England, institutionally the most anomalous and indeed anarchic of churches in the West, is in a better state than some.

Yet, in the long run, this fear is ill-founded. For the crumbling of the great monolithic religious organizations could result in the church regaining its necessary flexibility. Anarchy there may be in the sense that there will be no uniform pattern; chaos in that the patterns may have to continue to change with kaleidoscopic swiftness; serious mistakes are bound to be made; yet these conditions have always been indispensable for life, and to seek to inhibit them is self-defeating. The familiar imposed and all too readily accepted conformity is in fact a very superficial thing. Whether it conceals a deeper common life and faith, or substitutes for them when they are no longer there, the church is better without them. The fact that innumerable men and women have continued to find and live by the gospel through many long ages when the church seemed to stand for all that contradicted it, is due to the persistence of authentic elements of the Christian tradition, often in spite of those who have claimed to be the appointed guardians of it.

For if it is true that the church is not essentially a centralized organization, but is constituted by the presence of Christ in the eucharist, it follows that the local church is not a *part* of the church, but *is* the church in that particular place, and can be correspondingly sensitive to the shape and needs of its locality. And a Christian belongs to the church

76

in so far as he is a member of the eucharist. He will in the course of his life belong now to one group, now to another, or, as often happens today, to more than one group at the same time. Though in places it will be right to meet in churches, and even to build them, most groups will exist, unless they are artificially prolonged, for a time only, as circumstances demand. But this does not prejudice the continuity of the church, for the eucharistic assembly can never be static; it is continually dissolving and reconstituting itself, if not in one place, then in another – in 'field, desert, ship, inn, prison',[9] and nowadays other such places will come readily to mind.

The great merit of the sacramental model of the church is that it not only allows, but demands, that the church's outward forms should be appropriate to the context in which it lives, for only so can men recognize in it the presence of Christ. If Karl Rahner is right, and the church's task is not to bring the presence of Christ to the world, but to recognize that presence already there, to evoke it and to make it conscious and tangible, then the church can find its shape in every situation in which mankind exists. And to each such situation the church brings, not a predetermined order, not a policy or a propaganda (for it has nothing to sell), but a message, an interpretation, that says: 'Christ is here also, look and see him for yourselves; and if you will believe, here are his words and his signs – water, and bread and wine, by which you may live.'

The signs of Christ present at the centre of the church's life ensure, as nothing else can, that the church maintains its authentic stance in the world; that Christians sharing completely their fellow-men's concerns, can yet see them in another perspective and remain radically free in respect of them. For our world is in bondage, as much as the world of New Testament times ever was, to what are there called the 'principalities and powers',[10] and which we know as the forces that should serve man, but usually dominate him – the institutions he makes, public opinion, economic standards, religion, morality, political ideology, and that 'repressive tolerance' which whittles away a human being's inner capacity for criticism and reduces him, as Herbert Marcuse says, to 'one-dimensional man'.[11] From these powers man is liberated in Christ. This is the gospel, and of this gospel the church is to be the living sacrament.

NOTES

1. Leslie Paul, *The Deployment and Payment of the Clergy* (London: Church Information Office, 1964), p. 25.

2. *Epistle to Diognetus*, cf. p. 27.

3. Angus Wilson, *Late Call* (London: Secker & Warburg, 1964), pp. 191–4.

4. Charles Davis, 'The Church and the Churches', in *New Christian*, 22nd August, 1968, p. 10.

5. Cf. Esther de Waal, 'New Churches in East London in the Early Eighteenth Century', in *Renaissance and Modern Studies*, Vol. IX, 1965; for a pioneer study of this subject cf. E. R. Wickham, *Church and People in an Industrial City* (London: Lutterworth Press, 1957).

6. Harvey Cox, *The Secular City* (New York: Macmillan, and London: SCM Press, 1965), p. 45.

7. Quoted in John Coulson and A. M. Allchin, *Newman: A Portrait Restored* (London: Sheed & Ward, 1965), p. 15.

8. Cf. p. 20.

9. Cf. p. 56.

10. Cf. e.g. Eph. 6.12; Col. 2.15. For a full discussion of this subject and its contemporary relevance see Albert H. van den Heuvel, *These Rebellious Powers* (London: SCM Press, 1966).

11. H. Marcuse, *One-dimensional Man* (London: Routledge, 1964).

7 The End of Magic

Oskar, the midget anti-hero of Günter Grass's novel *The Tin Drum*, has wandered to the public park where there is to be a Sunday afternoon rally of the local Nazi Party. A platform has been put up, a rostrum, from which the speakers are going to address the crowd. Later his mischievous drum-beat will disrupt the proceedings by turning the military march of party members into a Viennese waltz. But now, looking at the platform before creeping underneath, he asks the reader:

> Have you ever seen a rostrum from behind? Everyone – if I may make a suggestion – should be familiarized with the rear view of a rostrum before being assembled in front of one. Anyone who has ever really looked at a rostrum from behind will be immunized at once, and be proof against any magic which, in one form or another, is practised on rostrums. Much the same can be said about the rear views of church altars; but that is another story.[1]

A new generation is rebelling against the 'powers', rebelling against being manipulated by politicians and managers and trade unionists, by universities and churches, by newspapers and advertisers. Underlying this protest is a disillusionment, in the strict sense of that word, and a consequent moral sensitivity which, among the uneducated and personally insecure, manifests itself in hooliganism and adolescent crime against a society hated as making deceptive promises. Among students it shows itself in a passionate concern for integrity, for intellectual and emotional honesty, whether it be in politics or economics, in the arts or sciences, or, above all, in personal relationships. Deeply suspicious of motives, this generation is impatient with authority in so far as authority is unwilling or unable to give its reasons. It is perfectly prepared to live with uncertainties and probabilities (and often steers an admirable course among them), but it is disposed to question all pre-packaged moral attitudes, whether they be patriotism, or the Ten Commandments.

The origins of this rebellion in a scientific attitude to knowledge and its application to our educational principles are not far to seek. For today we take it for granted that the process of being educated means learning to ask questions and testing the answers we are given against the evidence of experience. We find it hard to imagine a state of affairs in which education was predominantly a matter of being introduced to a received tradition and instructed in the implications which it should have for our lives. For us no traditional wisdom however venerable, no authority however august, carries weight without producing its evidence. And this is not because, unlike our forefathers, we are stubborn or unbiddable, but because, unlike them, we have to find our way in a world that confronts us at every step with a multitude of choices.

It is a situation which is bound to hold terrors for those who regret the values of Christendom and the older and simpler allegiance to God and his church, to King and country. They remember, or think they can remember, the contentment that came with the unquestioned acceptance of the Bible, of 'Christian' morality, and civilized behaviour. And, being older, they cannot assume (as they think the young too readily and naïvely do) that the values so hardly won in the past, such as the constitutional safeguards of civil liberties, are necessarily a permanent part of life and can be taken for granted. It is this fear that underlies the often irrationally violent reaction against the rebellious young which is now such a distinctive feature of Europe and America.

Yet it is not surprising that this old order of society should now appear to many to have been something of a conspiracy. To the rulers no doubt it seemed as if they were selflessly bearing the burden of decision on behalf of the common people. Plato could see no other way of ordering his Republic, and in state and church to this day good men have answered a vocation to shoulder this responsibility. From altar and from political platform the people have been bewitched, often indeed with both benevolence and beneficence, but the very fact it has been done 'for their own good', far from mitigating this manipulation, is just what makes it for them morally unbearable. Yet even if this may have been right and necessary once, it cannot be so now, if only because, for good or ill, the magic has been exposed. We have all seen behind the rostrum, we have all seen behind the altar, and have discovered them to be of imperfect and all too human construction after all. And so today every cultural consensus is seen as hypocritical, every myth as deceitful, every tradition as constricting.

But the difficulty is, of course, that every idea, if it is to be socially effective, *has* to be institutionally incorporated. And every institution, even any group, is bound to create its tradition, its mythology, its frame of reference, if it is to survive, and if the ideas it enshrines are to be communicated. The cultic heroes and vigorously asserted moral principles of the student revolt are themselves a case in point; as, more conventionally, is the consensus that upholds Parliament, for example, or the common law, or the university. And it is true for the church. What we have to find is a way of coming to terms with the inevitable and necessary magic involved in the living out of ideas, while keeping these ideas, and their incorporation in institutions, under a perpetual critical review. Hence the search for a new participatory democracy, or for a continuing reformation, the hope for a human society that genuinely rests on the consent of all its members.

Thus Peter Lennon wrote from Paris at the beginning of June 1968:

The atmosphere was one of youth taking the adult world tolerantly in hand and tactfully trying to civilize it. . . . Students put their case with gentle insistence. People came from all over the city to see what was going on, and got a little pep talk. . . . But quite a number finally caught on to the fact that what we were witnessing was the spectacle of the human animal as we would always like to see him – the imagination extended, physical courage, generosity, and optimism triumphing over the timidity, fear of insecurity, or just fear of discomfort, which keep our lives moving sluggishly. The fears, in fact, which cheat us out of part of the experience of living. That one great student slogan summed up the revolutionary attitude: take your dreams for reality.[2]

And writing at the same time Robert Stephens spoke of a 'revivalist movement'.

It is a search for more human relations in every form of activity, an attempt to avoid the bureaucratization of State as well as party and to remedy the dissociation of the public from the political system.[3]

Here the church's problem about its institutions and its structures is parallel to that of society at large. Or better, its problem is not parallel, it *is* the problem of man in society. This is what we should expect if what has been said in the last chapters about the nature of the church is true, if, as Karl Barth wrote, the church is 'God's provisional demonstration of his intention for all humanity'.[4] For many people, as we have seen, the church has itself been one of the powers, dominating and manipulating man, making him less rather than more fully human. The question is whether this is inevitable, whether the church as a human institution is, like other institutions so far, bound to grow to super-human proportions and employ a sub-human magic to make 'slaves' again of men who have once been called 'sons' and 'friends',[5] or whether it might contain in itself the seeds and the possibility of a new world.

This is the problem that Christian theologians have confronted in their centuries-long debate about tradition and authority.

To live in society, indeed to understand himself as a human being, man needs a frame of reference, something by which to interpret and order his experience. We saw that, in David Martin's analysis, 'Christianity' or 'religion' in an

82

enfeebled form still supplies such a frame of reference in England,[6] though there are signs today that it is breaking up, as the disintegration of a common culture, long sensed by the artist, is reaching consciousness in the popular mind. This frame of reference can variously be called a tradition, or, more technically, a mythology, where this word is not intended to judge the truth value of its constituent elements. It is a sort of communal history writing, a way that communities have in order to remain themselves, a way of exteriorizing their experience so that it may be shared and handed on. Such a tradition or mythology is very complex; it contains, for example, all those intangibles which make a particular nation conscious of itself as related to and yet distinct from other nations. It reflects man's many-sided relationships, all that unites him consciously and unconsciously with nature of which he is a part, with his physical environment, with other men and societies in past history. It is enriched by the creative and imaginative intelligence of members of his own society. It expresses itself in institutions and beliefs, in attitudes and customs, in morality and manners. And none of these elements act in isolation from one another; they influence each other and are mutually interpretative.

A tradition in this sense will almost certainly have elements in it that we would call legendary, stories that have become embroidered in the telling, even stories that originally belong somewhere else, but have become attached to particular persons or events in the tradition where they seemed appropriate; and, of course, the whole will have a slant, a bias, which selects favourable elements and rejects contradictory ones, both in large matters and in details. It is, for example, remarkable how far school textbooks of all countries will go to build up and to preserve the mythology of a nation. Thus it is said that much hostility to England among Americans stems from the fact that their first knowledge of the English is in terms of the oppressor, overthrown by the glorious Revolution; and, also in America, the legendary but extremely powerful myths associated with the original Constitution, or later with the Frontier, are well known to historians; and again, there is a so-called 'American way of life'. When I was at Harfleur in Normandy some years ago, the church bells rang out one day in honour of the 'hundred men of Harfleur' who, in the Hundred Years' War, had pushed an English army back into the sea. I had never heard of them; but then neither had my French hosts heard of Crécy, Poitiers, and Agincourt!

Nevertheless, it is important to observe that a tradition is still necessarily anchored in history. There *was* an American Revolution, and Constitution, and Frontier. The battles between the English and the French armies to which I have referred *were* fought. The existence of the nations themselves is sufficient testimony to the historicity of their origins and their growth, however much those facts have been coloured by interpretation and legendary accretion.

In these respects the tradition of the Christian church is bound to have characteristics similar to that of other human communities. It, too, reflects the complex relationships which man has with his environment, both natural and historical; it, too, has expressed itself in specific institutions, creeds, and ethics. It, too, has its distinctive perspectives. And, as we saw in Chapters 3 and 4, it also in its images unites him to man's universal experience of himself as part of nature and society. We would expect, therefore, that the Christian tradition, too, contained legendary materials and accretions that men have added in periods of uncritical enthusiasm or credulity. But the very existence of the church indicates that it did have origins in which historical people and events played their part, and the earliest records that we have show at least what kind of people and events these must have been to produce the church they portray.[7]

In accepting the Jewish canon of scripture, the Old Testament, the early church expressed its conviction that it could only understand itself in the historical context of God's providence, and thus included in its tradition a permanent element by which it could correct itself. This element was amplified and reinforced by the forming of a New Testament canon also, in which the church, rejecting as far as it could all that was patently legendary and spurious about Jesus, accepted only the testimony of those who could claim with some plausibility to speak of those things that they had heard, had seen with their eyes, looked on, and touched with their hands (I John 1.1). Inevitably it had to make its choice of documents according to what, by our standards, are very crude historical criteria, such as the ascription of apostolic authorship; but it was helped in its selection by other elements in the tradition – liturgy, early creeds, standards of Christian conduct, all still themselves relatively close to their origins – which together created a sense, a feel, of what was authentic and what was not. For the church, in securing its past memory of Jesus, referred to him also as it knew him in the Spirit in the present experience of its communal life. Particularly at the eucharist, when the scriptures, of both the Old and the New Testaments, were read, and when Christians, offering themselves to their Father, knew themselves to be united with Jesus and accepted in him, they saw themselves, their personal life and the corporate life of their tradition, in his light, and were inspired and judged by it. The scriptures were more than a collection of foundation deeds; the historical man of whom they spoke was the living word (I John 1.1). Jesus himself, 'the same yesterday and today and for ever' (Heb. 13.8), in so far as he was present in the church in his Spirit, preserved the authenticity of the tradition and continued to mark it with his perspective. Thus, as we saw, the early Christians did not believe in the Holy Spirit and in the church separately, but confessed their faith in 'the Holy Spirit in the Holy Church'.

We have also seen how, particularly in the West, as the liturgy moved from the house-church and became a matter of large-scale public worship, the communal life of the church declined. When later, in addition, the scriptures remained untranslated, the church in the common experience of its members was deprived of the controlling elements in its tradition. Both became the arcane preserve of the clergy; the mass was their individual affair, and of the Bible the medieval carol sang, 'as clerkes finden written in *their* book'.[8] And so the tradition became increasingly distorted, and the church, in losing the perspective of Jesus in its own life, lost also its specific stance towards the world.

This distortion is shown clearly in the change that comes about in the concept of authority in the church.

There can be for man no other authority than that of truth, which he experiences, in his reason and in his imagination, as a self-authenticating gift, and which calls from him an openness, an integrity, and an honest sensitivity in all his activities, whether they be intellectual, aesthetic, or moral. But just as a man can only apprehend truth in the categories, the whole cultural framework, in which the particular society he lives in interprets the experience provided by his senses, so also is his response to truth shaped by the community of which he is a part. Thus the universities are passionately concerned to protect their freedom from political or commercial pressures, and scholars in general feel themselves part of an international community which transcends the pettier interests of their particular countries.

For man to live under the authority of truth it is vital that the society in which he lives is itself prepared to live under that authority, and to let itself be judged by it. The relationships which constitute it must be informed by a mutual respect and honesty, a common humility before truth, which make it better to speak of the truth possessing man, rather than of man possessing the truth. And when a decision has to be reached in a particular matter, it is the truth that is seen to be authoritative, not the person or persons to whom it falls to voice the decision. The authority of truth demands an interior consent, not an external conformity.

For a Christian the truth, as it relates to the meaning of

his life, is illumined above all in Jesus, the Jesus that meets him in the tradition of the church. So Christians have spoken of the Spirit of truth who bears witness to Jesus and will lead them into all truth, and of the church as 'the church of the living God, the pillar and bulwark of the truth', in which they may discover the appropriate moral response to the truth thus revealed.[9] Christians are exhorted to *do* the truth (I John 1.6), to let the truth work in the ambivalences of their human relationships to produce that quality of integrity, that selfless and yet self-fulfilling love for which the New Testament, reflecting on Jesus, had to find a new word, *agape*, 'charity'.

It is in this love that in the church men speak the truth to one another (Eph. 4.15); in this charitable collaboration in which only authoritative decisions can be made that truly express the *consensus fidelium*, the participation of all the Christian people in the tradition. The word used by Russian Orthodox Christians, *sobornost*, best describes this common expression of the church's life; not readily translatable, it comes from the word for assembly or synod, and is applied to corporate worship as well as corporate authority; and it contrasts both with the authoritarianism of Rome and the individualism of Protestants.[10]

The beginnings of a change in the concept of authority in the church, which finally resulted in authority being understood as the power of ecclesiastical princes ruling, as God's representatives, over their subjects, can already be seen in the second half of the second century. In the course of controversy with the gnostics, who claimed to have a secret tradition of their own, the idea arose that the genuineness of the traditional order of life and faith could be shown by drawing up lists of successive leaders in each local church from the time of the apostles, symbolizing and, in a way proving the fidelity of that church to what it had received. In fact many of the earlier names on these lists are almost certainly not those of bishops in the later sense, but were so construed in the desire to discern a uniform order in the very fluid situation of the first century and the beginning of the second.[11]

From this developed, step by step, the notion that popes and bishops have received by delegation from Christ through the apostles the authority in their own persons to determine the tradition, and to be the source of the church's order. This view persists in the papal claims, and whenever bishops reserve to themselves the final judgment, whatever the state of their own knowledge about a matter, theological or otherwise; and also when churches not governed by bishops have been refused recognition, in spite of their faithfulness to scripture, creeds, and Christian life, because they are not regarded as possessing genuine ministries and sacraments.

In the papal claims we may see a development from the time that communion with Rome was, because of the universally recognized orthodox tradition of that famous church, a reliable test of orthodoxy, to the position, adopted later by the church of Rome itself (but understandably never accepted outside its sphere of influence), that orthodoxy was to be equated with obedience to the Roman bishop. And so as men have taken on themselves to exact obedience to their judgment of the truth, there follows that search for those elusive guarantees that will say in advance whether a particular decision is infallible or not; a search that is bound to be vain, because it is the truth that has the last word, and it is man who is judged.

This distortion of the Christian tradition was made all the more possible by the fact that for centuries in the so-called Dark Ages the church lived in a closed society – a society, that is, in which Christianity was the only world-view. In such circumstances any tradition comes to be thought of, not as one among several alternative interpretations of man's experience of reality, but as reality itself; and this makes self-criticism impossible, as there is, so to speak, nowhere outside the tradition for a man who would criticize to stand. More, as reality itself seems to be in question, criticism is in fact bound to be felt as a threat of ultimate chaos, and to be feared and resisted accordingly. The church, having forfeited its inner criterion of self-criticism, was thus deprived also of criticism from outside; and it came to accept its tradition, as it had actually developed to that particular moment in history, as absolute, to regard it as an inviolable sacred order. Christians took it for granted that the church had always been what it then was, a conviction that is strikingly evident in the Christian art and devotion, as well as in the theology, of the period. Yet, as Robin Horton writes:

> In each generation, small innovations, together with the process of selective recall, make for considerable adjustments of belief to current situations. But where they cannot refer back to the ideas of a former generation 'frozen' in writing, both those responsible for the adjustments and those who accept them remain virtually unaware that innovation has taken place. In a similar manner, a small and seemingly marginal innovation in belief can occur without anyone realizing that it is part of a cumulative trend which, over several generations, will amount to a very striking change.[12]

In the church's case, there *were* ideas of a former generation 'frozen' in writing, but, as we saw, these were nullified by the neglect of the scriptures, and by the fact that the small literate élite was psychologically disposed to force its own interpretation on both the scriptures and the writings of the early Fathers, so that the existing order of things should not be imperilled. Scripture in fact was now used in a new way, it became merely a source-book of divinely guaranteed proof texts to bolster independently constructed theological systems.

As a result of the invention of printing and the great spread of literacy at the end of the medieval period, men became aware of the contrast between the contemporary church and the church of earlier times; and the change in many respects was clearly one of corruption. In addition, the Western exploring and trading nations were coming into close contact with people of other cultures. On the Mediterranean there were cities in which Christian, Jewish, and Islamic communities lived side by side; and later, tales from the Americas, India and China further confronted the tradition of Western Christendom with alternative views of the world.

To talk of reform therefore no longer seemed to threaten the ultimate and sacred order of the universe, and came to be seen as both conceivable and urgent. Referring themselves constantly to the newly printed Bible, and to a lesser extent to the early Fathers, the sixteenth-century Reformers tried to re-establish criteria by which the tradition of the church might judge itself. Thus a 1571 canon of the English Convocations laid down that only that doctrine was to be believed which 'is agreeable to the teaching of the Old and New Testaments and has been gathered from that teaching by the catholic Fathers and ancient bishops'. Faithfulness to the authentic tradition reasserted itself as the criterion of truth, in the place of obedience to Rome, a church which was deemed to be capable of error like any other,[13] and we find Archbishop Cranmer, convinced that its corruptions were a hindrance to reform, praying daily that his church 'might be separated from that See'.

At the most, however, the intentions of the Reformers were only imperfectly realized, principally because the identification of church and society was still virtually complete, though now each nation might have its own religious settlement. Whereas the Reformers had hoped for a church perpetually reforming itself in the light of the gospel, their work resulted in the division of Christendom into a number of rival institutions, each using the scriptures in the medieval way to justify its own system and each attempting to trace its order back to the New Testament by what now appear to be tenuous links, dubious proofs, and question-begging arguments. Though reform was necessary, and indeed was soon paralleled in the Counter-Reformation, neither the new Protestant churches nor the new Roman Catholic Church effectively reintegrated the tradition, but kept the questioning perspective of scripture at a safe distance from their actual church life.

This resulted, in Protestantism, in further fragmentation when enthusiasts in the course of time were moved in the name of scripture to challenge the established church orders. The Roman Catholic Church, because it continued to regard its current structures and doctrinal formulations as irreversible, was faced with the problem of how to account for the immense changes that had become evident between the church as it now was and as it used to be. And the repeated attempt has been made by some of its best theologians to find the seeds of the present in the scriptures, while at the same time canonizing the process of development itself. But it is difficult to see how any doctrine of development can be convincing, remaining, as it must, merely descriptive of what has in fact developed, and neither explanatory of why this has developed and not that, nor predictive of what will develop in the future.[14]

In an increasingly open society, Christians are necessarily conscious again that the tradition of the church as it has come down to them is but one of a number of alternative interpretations of reality. One of the reactions to this, as we have seen, is nostalgia, a nostalgia that has in it a hard core of fear and results in turn in a frightening obscurantism, a refusal to look at the whole of life. This can take the form of compassing sea and land to make a single proselyte, and when he is one, making him twice as much a child of hell as oneself (Matt. 23.15); for every convert momentarily assuages doubt. This was certainly one motivation of Christian missions in the fifteenth- and eighteenth-centuries, as a closed society sought to protect itself against alien world views beginning to press on it,[15] and it is a common phenomenon today. More generally it shows itself in a man's dividing his mind into separate compartments, a glossing over of contradictions, which is all the more deadly for being often well-intentioned. The effect of this in Christianity is a blunting of the edge of thought in cliché, and that progressive

91

withdrawal of the church from reality which must lead to its eventual suffocation.

The other reaction is a return to humility. In the article already quoted, Robin Horton writes that in a closed society

> what the anthropologist almost never finds is a confession of ignorance about the answer to some question which the people themselves consider important. . . . Indeed it is only in a culture where the scientific attitude is firmly institutionalized that one can hope to hear the answer 'we don't know' given by an expert questioned on the causes of such a terrible human scourge as cancer. . . . From one angle, then, the development of the scientific outlook appears more than anything else as a growth of intellectual humility. . . . This humility, I suggest, is the product of an underlying confidence – the confidence which comes from seeing that one's currently held beliefs are not the be-all and end-all of the human search for order.[16]

The Christian no longer holds the tradition *as it now is* to be sacred. His confidence is in the truth, a truth which is not his to dispense but which, on the contrary, holds him with a grip that will not let him go. And so he is driven back to his sources.

In the revival of the liturgy, of the penetrating word and common life of the eucharist, there is the possibility that the church will recover its distinctive perspective. Certainly already there have sprung up many new and diverse groups, groups that correspond much more to the house-church of early times, and which are proportionate to the intrinsic demands of an effective ministry of word and sacrament.[17] In some places existing congregations are becoming again one or more groups of this kind; others arise among people with common concerns, in industry, in universities, in social work, or simply round a number of families and their network of friends. And there are many new institutes and associations of Christians, some more permanent than others, to do with education and writing, and with economic and social problems of every sort. In so far as they have already proved explosive of the present organized structures of the churches, have questioned central authority and increasingly disregarded denominational frontiers, the promise to be seen in such groups may prove to be real.

The question is whether the age-old mould of authoritarian systems has left enough life, substance, and wholeness in the Christian tradition to preserve its authenticity, once the centralized structures crumble or are repudiated; or will the tradition fragment and proliferate in a multitude of syncretisms, as has already happened to much of African Christianity?[18] An imperial power, as it is forced to withdraw, may rightly fear that a newly independent people is not ripe for self-government. Newman was surely right, more than a hundred years ago, to insist again and again on the priority of education and to see that the old church structures were not adequate for this.[19]

In the article quoted earlier, Robert Stephens spoke of 'the students' grasp of the revolutionary role of education' and

the attempt to break down the whole concept of the separation of learning and work, to replace the idea of education as a 'preparation' or 'qualification' by the concept of a perpetual renewal and interchange between education and the working world.

This is part of the 'demystification' due to

a widening access to the technical means of cultural production – such as cameras, tape-recorders radios – which for long remained virtual monopolies of mandarin groups, as learning once was of the monasteries.

And Marshall McLuhan has argued with some plausibility that the forms that man's civilizations take are primarily determined by the means of communication at his command, and suggests that just as the invention of printing effected a profound change in European culture, which has since spread through the world, so the new mass media, particularly television, will have a similarly far-reaching effect.[20]

Education, as was suggested at the beginning of this chapter, is the main weapon at man's command in his exposure of the magic practised by the powers that threaten

93

him. And it is no accident that at its best the church, wherever it has gone, has brought the means of education with it, for even if literacy was primarily thought of as a necessary condition for reading the scriptures, the Bible when allowed to speak for itself has always challenged the systems of men. This is why the church has a stake in an open society and in the promotion of that scientific approach to knowledge which an open society makes possible. Or better, the very purpose of the church necessarily involves the creation of such a society and the struggle to keep it in being and to extend it. For this open society is precarious. The 'religion' left over from Christendom still has its power, as can be seen in the ideology of 'Western European Christian civilization' which motivates the politics of many European, American, and white-dominated African countries. And in a technologically complex world many men are ready to submit to the new mystification of 'scientism' with as much credulity, expressed in a faith in inevitable 'progress', and lack of personal responsibility as to any older religion.[21] Edmund Leach's warning that this responsibility is inescapable may well fall on deaf ears.[22] The mass media themselves are only too liable to be used not to educate men, but to enslave them.

The church exists for just this: to enable men to live by Jesus' victory over the 'powers',[23] delivering them from slavery and enabling them by his Spirit to appropriate the freedom and qualities of his sonship[24]; to evoke, wherever men are, a community that lives in the openness and fidelity of friendship, in mutual respect and forbearance, in *sobornost*, in humility under the judgment of truth.

NOTES

1. Günter Grass, *Die Blechtrommel*. My translation. Cf. *The Tin Drum* (London: Penguin, 1965), p. 114.
2. *The Guardian*, 3rd June, 1968.
3. *The Observer*, 26th May, 1968.
4. Quoted in H. Cox, *The Secular City*, p. 145.
5. Cf. John 15.13–15; Rom. 8.14f; Gal. 4.7–9.

6. Cf. pp. 15.

7. For a full treatment of this theme see T. G. A. Baker, *What is the New Testament?* (London: SCM Press, and New York: Morehouse-Barlow, 1969).

8. *Adam lay ybounden*, fifteenth-century.

9. Cf. John 15.26; 16.13; I Tim. 3.15.

10. Cf. F. L. Cross (ed.), *The Oxford Dictionary of the Christian Church* (London: Oxford University Press, 1957), 'Sobornost'.

11. Cf. W. Telfer, *The Office of a Bishop* (London: Darton, Longman & Todd, 1962), pp. 107 ff.

12. Robin Horton, 'African Traditional Thought and Western Science', in *Africa*, Vol. XXXVII, Nos. 1 and 2, Jan. and April 1967, p. 180. My indebtedness in these paragraphs to this article is considerable.

13. *Articles of Religion*, XIX.

14. Cf. Owen Chadwick, *From Bossuet to Newman: The Idea of Doctrinal Development* (Cambridge University Press, 1957).

15. Cf. Robin Horton, *op. cit.*, p. 184.

16. *Op cit.*, pp. 173–5.

17. Cf. p. 56f.

18. Cf. G. C. Oosthuizen, *Post-Christianity in Africa* (London: C. Hurst, 1968).

19. Cf. p. 74.

20. Cf. Marshall McLuhan, *The Gutenberg Galaxy* (London: Routledge, 1962); *Understanding Media* (London: Routledge, 1964); *The Medium is the Massage* (London: Penguin, 1967).

21. Cf. C. F. von Weizsäcker, *The Relevance of Science* (London: Collins, 1964), Chapter 1; and Robin Horton, *op. cit.*, p. 186.

22. Cf. Edmund Leach, *op. cit.*, pp. 2 ff.

23. Cf. p. 82; and pp. 77f.

24. Cf. Gal. 5.22 f.

8 The Unknown Men

Nurtured in the apocalyptic hopes of their age, the first Christians saw the event of Christ as an event of cosmic dimensions. The writer of the epistle to the Ephesians fastens on the idea of Jesus descending to earth (and he may have in mind also the further descent into Hades at his death) and of his ascension 'far above all the heavens' to make the point of his universal significance, 'that he might fill all things' (Eph. 4.9 f.). The ascension is not thought of in the New Testament as a culminating event setting the seal on the biography of Jesus – the 'living happily ever after' part of the happy ending of the resurrection. It is the pre-condition of the fulfilment of his catholic mission. So the Fourth Gospel represents Jesus speaking to his disciples, 'It is for your good that I am leaving you' (John 16.7); 'I tell you, he who has faith in me will do what I am doing, and he will do greater things still because I am going to the Father' (John 14.12). Luke interprets the events of Pentecost in the light of Joel's words, 'I will pour out upon everyone a portion of my Spirit' (Joel 2.28; Acts 2.17), and represents Jesus as saying, 'You will receive power when the Holy Spirit comes upon you, and you will bear witness for me . . . to the ends of the earth' (Acts 1.8). Jesus' transit through the cosmos, from height to depth and from depth to height, is the work of a pioneer (Heb. 12.2); its significance that all the earth is ready to be filled with the sound of his words (Rom. 10.18), all things potentially subject to him (I Cor. 15.24–7). As Moses from the summit of Pisgah surveyed the promised land and charged Joshua to possess it (Deut. 3.27 f.), so Jesus on the Galilean mountain speaks:

All authority in heaven and earth has been given to me. Go therefore and make disciples of all nations, . . . and I am with you always (Matt. 28.16–20).

Quoting from the same passage from Joel, Paul wrote, 'For everyone who calls upon the name of the Lord will be saved' (Joel 2.32), and goes on to ask a series of rhetorical questions:

> But how are men to call upon him in whom they have not believed? And how are they to believe in him of whom they have never heard? And how are they to hear without a preacher? And how can men preach unless they are sent? As it is written, 'How beautiful are the feet of them that preach the gospel of peace, and bring glad tidings of good things!' (Isa. 52.7; Rom. 10.13–15).

Implicit in Christ's exaltation is that

> grace was given to each of us according to the measure of Christ's gift. . . . And his gifts were that some should be apostles, some prophets, some pastors and teachers, for the equipment of the saints, for the work of the ministry, for building up the body of Christ, until we all attain to the unity of the faith and of the knowledge of the Son of God, to mature manhood, to the measure of the stature of the fullness of Christ (Eph. 4.7, 11–13).

John Knox, writing about the event of Christ, his coming and his work, has emphasized that it is impossible to distinguish this from the emergence of the church; they happened together as, from the very beginning of his ministry, a group of disciples began to form round Jesus, a group whose character was then indelibly stamped by the events surrounding the crucifixion. The crucifixion happened 'under Pontius Pilate', a historical fact which is important, but its meaning, revealed in the resurrection, wholly belongs to the community, and is only perpetuated in the community.

> The only difference between the world as it was just after the event and the world as it had been just before is that the church was now in existence. A new kind of human community had emerged; a new society had come into being. There was absolutely nothing else besides. This new community held and prized vivid memories of the

event in which it had begun. It had a new faith; that is, it saw the nature of the world and of God in a new light. It found in its own life the grounds – indeed, anticipatory fulfilments – of a magnificent hope. But the memory, the faith, and the hope were all its own; they had neither existence nor ground outside the community. . . . The sole residuum of the event was the church.[1]

When, therefore, we speak about the Christian tradition, and the whole complex of memories, beliefs, and practices of which it consists, we can see that at the outset this tradition lived only among a small group of people, and that, as they went out from that group, its individual members were, so to speak, the sole bearers of it.[2] It is in this sense that the original apostles and prophets are authoritative. They are, in our current use of the word, authorities. They, no one better, know their subject. Thus when Luke recounts the story of the replacement of the traitor among the Twelve, Peter says:

So one of the men who have accompanied us during all the time that the Lord Jesus went in and out among us, beginning from the baptism of John until the day when he was taken up from us – one of these men must become with us a witness to his resurrection. (Acts 1.21f).

And it is on these grounds that all the New Testament writings implicitly, and many of them explicitly, seek to commend themselves.[3] For Paul to be able to speak with authority it is vital that his vision of Jesus on the Damascus road is accepted as a resurrection appearance, and it is to this that he devotes the opening chapters of his letter to the Galatians, where his authority is in dispute.[4] For this reason the apocryphal writings, however late, claimed to originate from the first disciples; and, as we have seen, in the formation of the canon of the New Testament, the criterion of genuine apostolic authorship was applied as far as was then possible.

The way in which apostolic authority is exercised is instructive. 'But we have this treasure in earthen vessels, to show that the transcendent power belongs to God and not to us' (II Cor. 4.7). So that their message may speak for itself, God has made the 'apostles last of all', they are 'fools for Christ's sake', 'the refuse of the world, the offscourings of all things' (I Cor. 4.9–13). Paul earns his own keep so that he can 'make the gospel free of charge, . . . for though I am free from all men, I have made myself a slave to all, that I might win the more . . . . I have become all things to all men. . . . I do it all for the sake of the gospel, that I may share in its blessings' (I Cor. 9.18–23). 'For what we preach is not ourselves, but Jesus Christ as Lord, with ourselves as your servants for Jesus' sake' (II Cor. 4.5). Throughout his letters Paul, confident that he speaks truly, yet sets out not to command but to persuade.

> We are ambassadors for Christ, God making his appeal through us. We beseech you on behalf of Christ . . . working together with him, we entreat you. . . . We put no obstacle in any one's way, so that no fault may be found with our ministry, but as servants of God we commend ourselves by great endurance. . . . We are the unknown men whom all men know. . . . Poor, we make many rich; penniless, we own the world (II Cor. 5.20–6.10).

Those who help Paul and continue his work, such as Timothy and Titus, are authoritative in a similar way. Often they are his first converts in a particular place and so are charged with building up the church, handing on all that they have received. Paul urges recognition for Stephanas and his fellow-workers, the first converts of Achaia, because 'they have devoted themselves to the service of the saints' (I Cor. 16.15–18). And to the Thessalonians he writes, 'We beseech you, brethren, to respect those who labour among you in the Lord and admonish you, and to esteem them very highly in love because of their work. Be at peace among yourselves' (I Thess. 5.12f). These men have not been instituted to any office. As in the case of the apostles they are authorities in so far as they have given themselves to the gospel, and are recognized accordingly.[5]

Nevertheless, here are the seeds of office. Paul had written 'Be at peace among yourselves'. This reconciling peace was at the heart of the gospel, and it inspired his conviction that there was only one faith, one baptism, one Spirit, one body, one eucharist, that the church was one because Christ could not be divided. This was a conviction on which he had staked everything. It led him into controversy with Peter, and motivated the immense labour of the collection among the Gentile churches for the poor of Jerusalem.[6] This same conviction led the churches later in the first century, and in the second, to collect Paul's letters, to circulate the Gospels, to formulate the first creeds, and to insist on the retention of all the Jewish scriptures. In this way the unity of the church was to be expressed by the unity and integrity of the Christian tradition. And gradually this unity came also to be reflected in a uniform pattern of ministry in the individual churches, until by the later second century all the churches that we know of were led by a single bishop and a number of presbyters and deacons.

From the outset, long before such official ministries crystallized, we can see Paul's anxiety for unity among the different churches, paralleled by a similar concern for harmony and order in the individual churches themselves. Because, as we have seen, that men may live under the authority of truth, may find and preserve their wholeness and human dignity, they need to belong to a community whose life is informed by those qualities of mutual love which Paul himself named the fruit of the Spirit (Gal. 5.22 f.).

This concern for order is manifest throughout the New Testament. It is not a desire for social conformity, nor is it the inculcation of subservient behaviour, of what Nietzsche stigmatized as the Christian slave morality, by attending to which a man might hope to save his soul. Nor is the strict watch repeatedly enjoined on Christians, lest their passions and appetites master them, rooted in a despising of the body. It is motivated rather by the knowledge that these can lead a man out of the community in which only his freedom can be found, and may indeed threaten to destroy the community altogether.[7] Paul warns the Corinthians against incest, but also (though admittedly less passionately) against disrupting the assembly by speaking in unintelligible tongues. And marriage is commended as a way of ordering the relations between the sexes in love; it reflects the self-giving love of Christ for the church. Again, the virtues most frequently insisted on in the accounts of Jesus' life and doctrine are the refusal to judge others, forgiveness, and a readiness to return good for evil, all of which, by breaking the blinding circle of retaliation, make it possible for true relationships to assert themselves.[8] Thus the peace commended in the New Testament is not a smothering of realities, but a positive prerequisite for integrity in human relations, and Paul's appeals for harmony in the churches to which he is writing have to be interpreted in the light of his concern for an order, as of a body in which each member is able to contribute his own aptitudes.[9] The moral renewal of man, of which baptism and the eucharist are signs, can only be perfected in the community and, as we saw, it is for this reason that each Christian makes his own self-oblation as a participant in the offering of the whole church.[10]

In fact the eucharistic assembly well exemplifies the ordering of a society in which each is valued for himself. Clement of Rome, writing towards the end of the first century, and speaking of different Christian ministries under Old Testament figures, exhorted the Corinthians in the following words:

> The high-priest has been given his own proper liturgies, and to the priests their special place is assigned, and the levites have their own ministries. The lay man is bound by the ordinances for the laity. Let each of you, brethren, make eucharist to God according to his own order, keeping a good conscience and not transgressing the appointed rule of his liturgy, and with reverence.[11]

Here the ministry of the church is one in which all are ordered, all participate according to their abilities, so that the community is itself a sign of right order in the world.

This communal character of the ministry assumes that the

local church is of a size in which men can genuinely meet and know one another. And certainly it is this family or house-church that Paul takes for granted in his letters, and which features repeatedly in Acts and elsewhere in the New Testament.[12] The Christian community, like any group, is bound to make use of the talents within it in order to fulfil its own inner needs and to respond to the outside pressures to which it is subjected. Some of these will be perennial, and this is doubtless the origin of the more permanent offices in the church, some will change; but every member of the community will contribute where his gifts lie, and leadership will pass from one to the other according to the particular demands of the moment.

This leadership never exists in its own right. Because its genesis and its purpose is to enable the group to be itself, it is bound to reflect the concerns and characteristics of the group. The church's more permanent leaders, when their offices came to be established, have had neutral titles. Bishop, presbyter, and deacon mean no more than overseer, elder and servant: today we might say chairman, committee member, and secretary or treasurer. They have taken on their colour, their richness of significance, from the nature and purpose of the church itself. If they speak with authority, it is to voice the common mind of the church, which is safeguarded by that rule of faith 'which admits neither increase nor diminution, by the reading of the scriptures without falsification . . . and by the special gift of love, which is more precious than knowledge, more glorious than prophecy, surpassing all other spiritual gifts'.[13] If they teach, it is the church's perception and knowledge they set forth, whether they be bishops, catechists, prophets or theologians, or any mother instructing her children. If they are pastors, it is because of the mutual care that Christians have for one another and for all that are in need. If they are priests, it is because the community is a sign of reconciliation among men in truth and justice, and because this community offers itself in thanksgiving through Christ to the Father.

102

Conversely, if the corporate life of the church is anaemic or false, the claims of its leaders to exercise these functions will appear pretentious, and take on an air of unreality.

When ceremonies of ordination to particular offices began, and what forms they took, are questions to which it is impossible to give certain answers, but they cannot have been less varied in the first century than the life of the scattered churches themselves. What evidence there is, and the known practice of later times, suggest that a community chose a man whose personal qualities and sound doctrine it respected,[14] laid hold of him or laid hands on him,[15] and prayed that God would endorse this choice by enabling him in the Spirit to fulfil and persevere in his calling. Thus ordination presupposed a double vocation: directly from God, in the sense that he has endowed a man with certain gifts, and from the church, in its selection of him to exercise particular functions; for the church, except at its worst moments, has never acted as if the grace of ordination were a substitute for natural aptitudes.

No more was implied than this; but also, if we reflect, no less. For this community believed itself to be the living body of Christ, the assembly in which he is present by his Spirit, and so ordination may rightly be called a sacrament, and those ordained sacramental men. For it is Christ's gifts, perfecting their own, that they exercise, his word they speak, his body and blood they share among their brethren, his love, his care, his healing and forgiveness they mediate to men. Bishop Westcott, commenting on John 20.21, wrote:

The Lord presents His own Mission as the one abiding Mission of the Father; this He fulfils through His church. His disciples receive no new commission, but carry out His. . . . They are not (in this respect) His envoys, but in a secondary degree envoys of the Father.[16]

Likewise the ordination prayers of Hippolytus, at the beginning of the third century, ask that God may give to a new bishop the same 'princely' and 'high-priestly' Spirit that he had bestowed on Jesus; and that a deacon may 'minister' as Christ 'ministered'[17]. The diaconate is not referred to, as in the Anglican Ordinal, as an 'inferior office'! This same instinct has had a reciprocal effect on some New Testament writings, as when Jesus is called 'the Apostle and High Priest' (Heb. 3.1) or 'the Shepherd and Bishop of your souls' (I Peter 2.25).

The continuing concern for order in the churches resulted gradually in their principal function crystallizing in an official ministry, a process which is already evident in the passage quoted from I Clement. In some places the churches seem long to have been presided over by a group of presbyters, in some a single bishop may have emerged very early. St Ignatius of Antioch, who was martyred about AD 115, already insists on the bishop as a sign and test of unity in the local church:

> Let no man do aught pertaining to the church apart from the bishop. Let that eucharist be considered valid which is under the bishop or him to whom he commits it. Wheresoever the bishop appears, there let the people be, even as wheresoever Christ Jesus is, there is the catholic church.[18]

By the time of Hippolytus it is clear that all the ministries of the church coinhere in the ministry of the bishop: it is he who shepherds, presides at the eucharist, and at ordinations, forgives sins, exorcizes and heals.

At this point it is worth quoting again some words by Father Audet:

> If you invite a small number of relations or friends to your house, you will ask them to sit down at your table and you will yourself serve them. . . . If fifty people come you would alter the time of the occasion and would arrange for refreshments. . . . If two hundred people are invited you would put the matter into the hands of professional caterers and you would greet personally only some of your guests and make a little speech. . . .[19]

No parable could illuminate more clearly the way in which the form of the church's ministry has been shaped by the character of the church's life. Father Audet himself employs it to show how celibacy, which had originally suited the kind of life led by an itinerant apostle, came in course of time to attach to the status of the priestly celebrant of the sacraments in a large community, supplanting the head of the household whose function this used to be, and who would naturally be married. Two changes have taken place: a style of life appropriate to a particular task has become a mark of status; and a ministry founded on the natural leadership of a small group has become a profession. The professional caterers have taken over.

We can see that as a community grew there would come a moment when it could afford to support one or more of its members, so that they could have more time to exercise their functions. In the first instance a deacon who had care of the poor might well be such a person, or a bishop who had to devote much care to teaching. In the course of years, particularly when presbyters came to exercise individual responsibility by delegation from the bishop, what we now know as the clergy came into existence, a group of men who thought of themselves as a corporation with its own professional ethos. Already in the third century Christians began to complain that bishops were becoming unmindful of Jesus' words that those who would be first must be servants of all;[20] and later bishops and presbyters came to regard their authority in terms of personal power, received from Christ and the apostles by delegation when they were consecrated and ordained.

This notion of power dominated the medieval theology of the ministry, and it is far from dead. It is held, for example, that at the Last Supper Jesus delegated to his apostles his priestly powers of offering the sacrifice of the mass, a power that has come down by unbroken succession to validly ordained priests today.[21] At another time, it is said, Jesus gave them the power of granting or witholding absolution; at another time the authority to teach, the powers of the *magisterium;* at another time he gave specific power to Peter only. As far as delegation in succession to the apostles is concerned, the disputes between Roman Catholics and Anglicans have in the past centred, not on whether there has been in Hooker's phrase a 'lineal descent of power from the Apostles by continued succession of bishops',[22] but on the exact nature of this power, on whether Anglicans have this succession, and on the question whether or not the papal power is to be included in the same category. We have seen that this whole way of understanding the ministry is vitiated by the fact that the New Testament writers are not concerned with institutions in the later sense at all, and that Jesus himself eludes any pretentions on our part to comprehend him in our religious categories.[23] Yet it still underlies much contemporary theology of the church, and in particular any view which, recognizing the centrality of the sacraments to the church's life, makes these sacraments and thus the church itself depend wholly on the ministry.

The practical consequences of this distorted theology of the ministry are not far to seek.

(1) For a long time, both in the older churches and in the missions, the number of clergy available has been determinative of the number of congregations that exist, or at any rate of congregations that could hope to have the eucharist at the centre of their life. Half a century ago Roland Allen was already protesting against this, and urging that what he called a 'voluntary' ministry should be sought for, chosen by the congregations themselves, and making possible again a spontaneous expansion of the church in missionary situations.[24]

(2) The clergy have generally been deployed in the first instance to maintain existing structures, and many fields calling for an apostolic and prophetic ministry have been ignored.

(3) As a self-styled profession the clergy have been in modern times increasingly pushed to the periphery of society, because many of their former functions have been taken over by other educators and social workers. In England the notable increase, in the course of the nineteenth century, in the clergy's religious quality, their pastoral zeal, and devotion to prayer and learning, remarked on in Pro-

fessor Owen Chadwick's first volume on the Victorian church,[25] concealed the beginning of their removal from the centre and leadership of public life. In the face of this a 'clergy of the gaps' theology of the ministry has not been very consoling, though the inadequacies of the social services are real enough.

(4) A clericalist doctrine of the ministry has produced the curious phenomenon, much in evidence today, of what might be called an 'inverted' clericalism. There has been much writing about the so-called 'priesthood', 'apostolate', and 'leadership' of the laity, who are thought of as fulfilling their ministry in the 'real' world. The clergy are respectfully restricted to their studies and to the exercise of their 'sacramental powers', in order to provide the laity with a sort of spiritual canteen on Sundays. For all the excellence of its emphasis on the fact that every Christian has his ministry, such a theology makes a coherent account of leadership in the Christian community impossible, because it is precisely its leaders that the church has always ordained. If these leaders are now discovered to be cut off from 'reality', the remedy is not to find substitutes, but to seek an ordained ministry whose way of life is consonant with the world as it is.

Does this mean that there is no room in the church for a full-time, 'professional' ministry? The reply must be that in the complexity of our society no single answer is either possible or desirable, and that a return to an earlier doctrine of the ministry, going behind both clericalism and 'inverted' clericalism, could restore also an earlier spontaneity and flexibility. The view still prevails that the only ministry in the church is that of a parish priest, of a vicar or minister of a settled congregation, with opportunities for a few to be promoted to a higher spiritual bureaucracy. Yet, if we will discern them, the gifts of the ascended Christ are infinitely various, qualifying men both for work in their own communities as pastors and teachers, and calling them far as evangelists, prophets, and apostles.

NOTES

1. J. Knox, *op. cit.*, pp. 44 ff.

2. Cf. Acts 13.1–3.

3. Cf. Luke 1.2; John 19.35; 21.24; I John 1.1–4.

4. Cf. also e.g. I Cor. 9.1; 15.8.

5. Cf. J. Knox, *op. cit.*, p. 91.

6. Cf. I Cor. 1.12 f; 4.17; 10.2–4; 12.13; 14.33 f.; 16.1–4; Gal. 2.1–16; also Acts 15.1–29; Eph. 4.3–6.

7. Cf. e.g. Rom. 13.8–14; Gal. 5.16–25.

8. Cf. Matt. 5.38–48; 6.12–15; 7.1; 18.21 ff.; Mark 11.25; Luke 6.37; 23.34; John 12.47; I Cor. chs. 5 and 14; II Cor. 2.5–11; Eph. 5.21–33.

9. Cf. e.g. Rom. 12.3–16; I Cor. 1.10; chs. 12–14; I Cor. 13.11 f.; Gal. 5.20; 6.2–6; Eph. 4.1–16; Phil. 1.27; 2.2; Col. 3.12–15.

10. Cf. Chapters 3 and 4.

11. I Clem. 40.5–41.1.

12. Cf. Acts 2.2,46; 5.42; 12.12; 18.7; 20.8, 20; Rom. 16.5; Col. 4.15; I Tim. 3.4 f.; Philemon 2; also possibly Matt. 10.12.

13. Irenaeus, *Adversus Haereses* IV. xxxiii.

14. Cf. I Tim. 3.1–13; Titus 1.5–9.

15. For the meaning of 'laying-on-of-hands', cf. W. Telfer, *op. cit.*, pp. 187 ff.

16. B. F. Westcott, *The Gospel according to St. John* (London: Murray 1908), p. 359.

17. Hippolytus, *op. cit.*, 2,9.

18. Ignatius of Antioch, *To the Smyrnaeans* 8.1f.

19. Cf. Chapter 5, note 4.

20. Mark 10.42–45; cf. G. Bardy and others, *Prêtres d'Hier et d'Aujourd'hui* (Paris 1954), which is the most forthright study of clericalism that I know.

21. Thus in a Pastoral Letter on 'Vocations to the Priesthood' on 3rd November, 1968, Bishop Ellis, Roman Catholic Bishop of Nottingham, wrote: 'God has decreed that the merits of Redemption were to be applied to mankind only by means of a sacrificing priesthood and that this priesthood was to be handed down through the ages by ordination.'

22. R. Hooker, *Of the Laws of Ecclesiastical Polity*, VII. 14.11. Hooker himself argued that there might be exceptions to this rule.

23. Cf. Chapter 2.

24. Cf. David M. Paton (ed.), *The Ministry of the Spirit, Selected Writings of Roland Allen* (London: World Dominion Press, 1960).

25. Owen Chadwick, *The Victorian Church*, Pt. I (London: A. & C. Black, and New York: Oxford University Press, 1966).

9 Communications

If it is true, and the conclusion is inescapable,[1] that the only difference between the world as it was before Jesus Christ and the world as it was after him, is the existence of the church, we can see the grounds of the conviction, evident already in the early letters of Paul, that the churches should manifest, both in their life in each place and also between themselves, the agreement of love in the truth. 'Is Christ divided?', he asks rhetorically, knowing that only one answer is possible (I Cor. 1.13). Nearly three centuries later, St Athanasius was to write in the same vein, speaking of Christ's victory over death:

> Therefore it is also, that he neither endured the death of John, who was beheaded, nor was he sawn asunder like Isaiah: even in death he preserved his body whole and undivided, so that there should be no excuse hereafter for those who would divide the church.[2]

What came to be called the 'visible' unity of the church was recognized at the outset as implicit in the gospel of him in whom God was reconciling the world to himself (II Cor. 5.19).

In the later writings of the New Testament the urgency for unity among the churches has become a dominant theme. The epistle to the Ephesians, which is in fact a general epistle addressed to all the churches and may have been composed to preface the first collection of Paul's letters, refers, when it speaks of the church and of the body, not to a particular congregation but to the whole people of God. God, who has purposed to unite all things in Christ, is making this mystery known in the church, in which no men are to be strangers, but 'fellow-heirs, members of the same body, and partakers of the promise of Christ Jesus through the gospel' (Eph. 3.6). As there is one God and one Lord, so there is to be one hope and faith and baptism, one Spirit and one body.[3] The Gospel of Matthew, whose principal purpose is to collect and order the tradition of the church, and that of Luke, who avowedly sets out to write 'an orderly account of the things that have been accomplished among us' (Luke 1.1–4), both reflect this concern for unity; and Luke continues his narrative in Acts to suggest a regular pattern in the spread of the gospel from Jerusalem until Paul reaches the centre of the Empire of Rome. The Pastoral Epistles likewise set out to strengthen the common tradition in their emphasis on standards of faith and Christian conduct.

The whole is summed up in Jesus' prayer to the Father in John 17.

As thou didst send me into the world, so I have sent them into the world. And for their sake I consecrate myself, that they also may be consecrated in truth. I do not pray for these only, but also for those who are to believe in me through their word, that they may all be one; even as thou, Father, art in me, and I in thee, that they also may be in us, that the world may believe that thou hast sent me (John 17.18–21).

Particularly in these words may be discerned already that understanding of the church which later was expressed in the marks, 'one, holy, catholic, and apostolic'. The church is apostolic, sent into the world that all men might believe, sent because of the universal significance of Jesus' own mission; it is holy, it lives according to the truth (I John 1.6), dedicated to God as the old Israel was called to be, a dedication perfected in Jesus; it is catholic, for all men everywhere, of every race and class, touching all their lives, from whom through its word is evoked their own response of faith; above all it is one, one with that quality of love in which the Father committed all things to the Son,[4] and in which the Son returned obedience to the Father, one in the

110

Spirit who is that love, in a unity without which apostolicity and catholicity and holiness fail. Schism in the church is more than a sin, it is the manifestation of sin itself, the failure of love, and of the church.

Jesus' words are addressed to his disciples. But in his accounts of their commissioning, the author of the Fourth Gospel must certainly have had in mind those helpers and successors of the original disciples who were then labouring to achieve unity among the scattered communities, and who worked to maintain the tradition in the face of gnosticism and other attempts to adopt Christianity into the fashionable religions of the day.[5] We have seen already that Paul urged the churches which he had founded to respect such men,[6] and a similar concern underlies such sayings as, 'He who receives you, receives me, and he who receives me receives him who sent me' (Matt. 10.40), and, 'Whatever you bind on earth shall be bound in heaven, and whatever you loose on earth shall be loosed in heaven' (Matt. 18.18), or again when the promise of the keys of the kingdom is made to Peter (Matt. 16.19). These are good examples of the operation of selective recall in a tradition when, in order to maintain itself and solve present problems, it remembers (doubtless with some elaboration) appropriate incidents in its early history.[7] At this time, when the tradition was still very fluid and when little had been committed to writing, it was vital that the credentials of those who could claim to be authoritative should be established as vigorously as possible.

As the more permanent functions in the communities crystallized into official ministries, and especially when a measure of uniformity between the churches in this respect developed with the emergence everywhere of a single bishop, the attempt was made to formalize the role of authoritative men in the church. This was in some ways a parallel development to the compiling of the New Testament canon and the creeds.

The beginnings of the doctrine of apostolic succession, as we saw, can be traced to the idea that the genuineness of the

111

traditional faith could be shown by drawing up a list of successive leaders in each church from the time of the apostles.[8] It was assumed that the office of bishop had been instituted by the apostles, and so they became a symbol of the continuity of the tradition, and this was reinforced by their becoming the principal ministers of ordination. A complementary idea was that by presiding over the local church, and by meeting in council, representing the whole to the part and the part to the whole, the bishops, witnessing together to the tradition of the whole church, were also the sign and the means of its unity. After quoting Ephesians 4.4–6, St Cyprian, who was bishop of Carthage from 248 to 258, wrote:

This unity we ought firmly to hold and defend, especially we who preside in the church as bishops, that we may prove the episcopate to be itself one and undivided.[9]

It is for these reasons, and not because they hold 'that the very essence of the church's reality inheres in, or can be conveyed only through, the bishop's office',[10] that today episcopal denominations have urged, and many others have been in principle prepared to accept, that a reunited church should be an episcopal one. For so-called 'non-episcopal' churches have not been lacking in that ministry of oversight and order that belongs to the bishop's office; as in many churches in the first and second centuries, the same functions have been exercised among them in other ways.

So far, only in countries where Christians are minority groups have different denominations been prepared to consider what would be required of them, if they were to return to a pattern of episcopacy which approximates to that of the early church. Here the impetus has been greater and the obstacles fewer than in places where powerful rival establishments have long maintained themselves side by side, if not in overt opposition. Yet even here, in spite of the liberation that comes when particular traditions are questioned in a common return to deeper and more vital

112

roots, a fact generally admitted and admired in the case of the Church of South India,[11] the difficulties are enormous. The reason for this, if the argument of this book has any validity, is that the denominational organizations are not, properly speaking, churches at all, but structures that in effect subject the church to the world, in the sense that it is the world's values that the church is driven to uphold, and the world's values that it employs to promote and defend its own interests. Thus Bishop Stephen Neill has written:

> When all is said and done, the last and gravest hindrance to unity is simply the deep desire of the denominations to continue their own separate existence. This is frequently rationalized as a concern that there should be no diminution in the body of inherited truth. The tacit assumption is made that this truth can be safeguarded only as long as it remains in the guardianship of this particular denomination organized as it is at present. It is a well-known fact that the majority of the mentally ill are ill because they want to be ill – in some strange way their sickness is of value to them. If the desire to be ill could be replaced by a whole-hearted desire to get well, the patient could arise and walk – but at the price of losing whatever it was of value that was represented by the sickness. If the churches really wanted to be one, they could be one within measurable time; what holds them apart is in large measure the deep-seated love of separate existence, pride in valued traditions, and the sense of superiority enjoyed by those who feel themselves to have been endowed with a special portion of the truth.[12]

This 'mental illness' has little to do with those who are the church's leaders, for the church has rarely been served by men of such devotion and good will. The fact is that they, too, are enmeshed by the 'power' that the institutional church has become. This appears clearly whenever these same leaders are enabled to stand outside their own structures; in such circumstances they can speak with an entirely different voice, as happened notably at the World Council of Churches assembly at Uppsala in 1968. In the matter of church unity this same freedom was shown at the Faith and Order Conference of the British Council of Churches at Nottingham in 1964, in a notable resolution, overwhelmingly adopted and clearly expressing the deep

113

conviction of representative church leaders of all persuasions, and which nevertheless subsequently fell on entirely deaf ears:

> We ask our churches . . . to accept that, while we affirm standards of belief to be an essential element in the life of the church, our remaining differences concerning the use of these standards, and concerning the relation between Scripture and Tradition, though important, are not sufficient to stand as barriers to unity. They do not separate us at the point of the central affirmation of our faith, and they can better be explored within a united church.[13]

It was to be expected that at first the way to unity should have presented itself in the form of an amalgamation of businesses in competition with one another, beginning with those among them who had very similar wares to promote. Yet even then the prospect of one immense monopoly, a super-denomination, was appalling to many. Such a form of visibility of the one church seemed to them intolerable, and, as there appeared to be no other way, there were those who felt that Christians would have to settle for less than the ideal, that a variety of choice would oppress mankind less, though they were prepared to envisage a federal structure for consultation and action on some common problems.

But this was to misread the situation. The impetus of the ecumenical movement does not come from the central bureaucracies of the denominations, except in so far as they have felt themselves driven to seek comfort from one another in an unfriendly world, and to hold hands in the dark. On the whole when denominations have moved towards unity with one another, and few have gone further, this has been due to the labour within them of a few dedicated men and women. Yet time and again, even if they have been officially appointed to negotiate, they have met and reached agreement, only to be repudiated or ignored by their respective churches.

The pressure for unity has come from the increasing number of Christians who have found themselves part of that biblical and sacramental renewal of the church with which

114

the last chapters have been concerned, and who have discovered that this renewal is at work in all the churches irrespective of the old denominational boundaries. Because the church can be found, and its life lived, only in the eucharistic community of the local church, a Christian senses that the *whole* church is his, not that part only to which he happens to be denominationally connected. Moreover the local community is impelled to adapt itself to the shape of society and to find Christ there. And Christ is not divided. It is this which drives Christians to ignore, however reluctantly, the rules of their denominations about communion. They sense their allegiance to the whole church, manifested here in the local community where Christ in his Spirit is present among them. For them the old excommunications hurled at one another by their ancestors have little meaning, and little claim on their loyalty.

The consequences of this, and of countless friendships among Christians, moving more freely at home and travelling abroad, have been far-reaching. The discovery that in the course of long warfare, one's own tradition has become distorted, and that the beliefs of others have been caricatured; that 'there is no necessary connexion between upholding liberty of conscience and not caring what men believe'[14]; that infinitely more unites divided Christians than separates them; above all the realization that 'no man, no church, possesses the fullness of theological truth or ever will'[15]; all these have helped to break open the separate sub-cultures that the denominations have produced and that have served to perpetuate the denominations in their turn.

This does not mean that Christians whose traditions have long lived in isolation disinherit themselves when they meet. Often those traditions have manifested one aspect of catholicity, that aspect which, because the gospel speaks to the whole of man, has in the past led national churches in particular to penetrate the life of their country. Though the lack of catholicity's other aspect, that which transcends the

115

way of life of any one people, because the gospel is addressed also to all men in every epoch, has generally meant that the identification has been too complete. When separated Christians meet, therefore, they do bring with them much that is of value. But two things happen. One is that in the process of mutual enrichment and correction, a balance and wholeness is restored, a unity that is more than the sum of its constituent parts, and henceforth inexorably judges those parts. The second result is a return to theological humility, the knowledge that man can only see the truth darkly reflected in the glass of his own language, that not until he sees face to face will he know as he is known. This humility has led to the present difficult enterprise among Christians to distinguish what is of faith and what of theological interpretation, an enterprise that has been encouraged by the rediscovery of the rich variety of theology in the New Testament itself, by which the faith of the church may be nourished. Thus Hans Küng wrote:

It is only in the faith that the church must have unity, not in theology. One Lord, one faith, one baptism (Eph. 4.5), but not, one theology![16]

If one has lived in the closed world of a tradition – any tradition – it is, as we saw, all but inevitable that the inherited ways of formulating belief are identified with belief itself; one remains unaware that one is heir to a tradition at all. The regaining of criteria by which to discriminate between essentials and inessentials that the meeting of separated Christians brings, is part of the process in which, in an open society, Christianity as a whole is forced again to look to its sources in order to discover what it is. It is this last question which is prior to any ecumenical debate, and perhaps the greatest value of the ecumenical movement so far is that it has focussed this problem for Christians.

I have argued that if the church is to be a credible sign of the kingdom, the promise of a society in which man may find freedom and grow to his full potential, then it must solve for itself the question how such a community can be

116

sustained. And I have tried to show that the seeds of an answer may be found in a view of the church which sees it as evoking such a community in each place, in all the variety that 'locality' has come to assume for mankind. But to assert again the sacramental nature of the church, that its authority is the Spirit of truth who in the communal life of its tradition marks it with the characteristic stamp of Jesus, that its ministry is one in which all are ordered, means that one must face also the questions of unity with which the first generations of Christians wrestled. How is the wholeness of the tradition to be maintained, the unity of faith, so that men are not 'tossed to and fro and carried about with every wind of doctrine, by the cunning of men' (Eph. 4.14)? As in each separate place, so also in the world at large, the church must point a way to unity which does not press down on men, but liberates them in all the variety of their cultures, so that the order of all men in justice and peace may be visibly signified in the communion of the holy churches of God.

Is the way to such a unity, as Anglicans in particular are prone to argue, a general return to episcopal government? The implications of this suggestion reach much further than is frequently realized. The present bishops of the Roman Catholic Church and the Church of England, for example, can in no real sense be said to represent the local church to the church at large. They are not elected; they neither shepherd a congregation, nor preside at its eucharist, nor preach; at best on their itineraries, in Father Audet's words, they make a little speech and personally greet a few. Many of them even have more clergy than they can really know, or, which is just as important, than can really know them. Nor are many of them chosen because they are, in the original sense, authoritative about the Christian tradition. It is not surprising, when they reach a decision therefore, whether prayerfully by themselves or in council with other bishops, that they do not successfully represent the universal to the local church; for most of those affected by that decision have taken no part in its making.

117

In order to mitigate this, the attempt has been made in the last fifty years, particularly among Anglicans and recently also by Roman Catholics, to find a more representative structure for an episcopal church, so that the clergy and also the laity may have a voice in its government. Anglicans, not unnaturally, have adopted the parliamentary model of separate Houses for bishops, clergy and laymen, who debate and vote independently. As far as Roman Catholics are concerned, Bishop Christopher Butler has suggested that the papacy should be reformed on the lines of the British constitutional monarchy. In the controversy that followed the encyclical *Humanae Vitae*, in which a pope ruled on the matter of contraception, sincerely believing himself to be personally charged and empowered by God to make a decision for the whole of mankind, Bishop Butler said:

I would point out that it took generations to transform the English monarchy of the late Stuart period into our present constitutional monarchy. It would not have happened overnight. I want the Papacy to be far more like the English monarchy than like the Roman Empire. But what won the day for constitutional principles in England was that the people were prepared to go on fighting and struggling, generation after generation. That is what I hope will happen in the church.[17]

But today I think we must question whether any model on the lines of a pyramid provides an adequate political structure for society. This is the problem which confronts modern nations, both internally and internationally. The model of a pyramid, whether the summit is the all-powerful emperor, or whether he is reduced to a figure-head by a parliamentary or bureaucratic system at the level immediately beneath him, was appropriate in a time when communications were difficult and large masses of people were illiterate or uneducated. But now when men have seen 'behind the rostrum', 'behind the altar', they are no longer disposed to accept as authoritative those whose only claim to be heard is that they are *officially* in authority. It is not, as is often supposed, authority itself which is rejected. The truth is rather that increasingly in an open society men will accept only an authority which can give its reasons, which is authoritative in the sense that it presses on them interiorly.

We have therefore to ask whether our present church structures have necessarily to be the same as those devised by Christians in the second century? We take it for granted that our attitude to scripture and our knowledge of history is entirely different from theirs. That is not to say that for us scripture has no authority; or that the exposure of some elements in our tradition as legendary means that for us its foundations are no longer reliable. On the contrary, we would say that critical and historical study have helped us to make the same response of faith in our own terms that the first Christians made in theirs. And they have helped us also to rediscover the richness and the variety of the original tradition, and to unlearn much that over the centuries had grown to obscure it.

It is therefore far from unreasonable to question whether the forms of official ministry that were built up at that time are sacrosanct. By common consent they were not part of the original proclamation of the gospel by Jesus and the community that grew round him, but a subsequent response of the church to enable it to remain faithful to the gospel in the circumstances of its own day. It is fruitless to question whether or not those forms were appropriate then, but we have seen that it is hazardous to canonize the process of historical development in the tradition. For this the distortions which followed in later times are sufficient evidence. That some of these early institutions have in name survived to our own day must not blind us to the fact that they have changed in almost everything but name. To venerate the present form of the episcopate because we rightly venerate 'the catholic Fathers and ancient bishops' is anachronistic. The uniformity from the second century onwards of the official ministry, and the claims made for it later simply because it was official, must not be allowed to obscure the fact that from the beginning some men and some

119

churches, men such as Cyprian and Basil and Augustine, churches like Antioch and Alexandria and Rome, continued to be more authoritative than others. The most effective testimony in the church to its tradition has always come from Christians, some of them famous and many that are long forgotten, quite irrespective of their positions, though at its best the church has found such men to fill its offices, and still continues to do so. And we may well believe that God has raised some to high office in order that they might be heard. In this way, in our century also, Lambert Baudouin and Charles de Foucauld, Dietrich Bonhoeffer and Karl Barth, William Temple and John XXIII have spoken with Christianity's authentic voice. And every Christian could readily add many names of his own to such a list.

Karl Rahner, in the address already quoted, looks to a time when

> the bishop will not look very different from any other official in a small voluntary group. The Christian of the future will not feel himself reduced in stature or oppressed by his bishop. . . . It will be clear and plain to see that all dignity and office in the church is uncovenanted service, carrying with it no honour in the world's eyes. . . . Perhaps it will no longer constitute a profession at all in the social and secular sense.

And he predicts that the clericalism still evident in the doctrine of the collegiality of the bishops in the constitution *De Ecclesia* of the Second Vatican Council will give way to the more fundamental understanding that

> we are all one in Christ, that the ultimate difference is the degree of love for God and the brethren; that distinctions of office are necessary but entirely secondary and provisional, a burden, a service, a sacred responsibility.[18]

In an open world, when man discovers that the only authority under which he can live is the authority of truth, he looks for a structure of society whose relationships are informed by that same authority. And he finds that social structures are not in the first instance concerned with the exercise of power at all, of the coercive power that men then take to themselves, and wield over others. The structures of society have to do not with power, but with communication; they are means by which men may reach decisions that respond adequately to their common needs. Thus it is that the means of communication available to them will determine the shape of the structures they erect. The Christian councils and synods of the first centuries were authoritative, not because of who summoned them, or mysteriously because they *were* councils, but because the bishops that met there could rightly claim to speak for the tradition as it had been received in their churches, and corporately submitted themselves to the truth. And it was the people of God as a whole who subsequently judged whether or not the council spoke truly.

Such structures may still be, or might be again, appropriate in societies, of which there are many in Africa and Asia, whose means of communication are not unlike those of the West at an earlier period of its history. But in the complex industrial civilizations of Europe and America new ways of communication have become established, and it is these which are generally used to reach social consensus.

Robert Stephens, in the article already quoted, notices that

> technology, which in some cases demands large-scale organization and central control for its activity and comparable institutions – such as the Common Market – also makes a much greater decentralization possible in other ways. Modern communications can have the effect of restoring great autonomy to the individual or small group.[19]

The resentment of many politicians is sufficient evidence of the way in which television in particular is weakening the old political systems, and it is significant that it is newspaper offices and radio and television centres, and not Bastilles, that today's revolutionaries storm.

It may be that in our world the unity of the Christian faith may be ensured by television and travel, by centres of education and common work, by reading and by hospitality. Already these are largely the ways in which Christians both individually and in groups learn from one another and, enriched by the tradition as a whole, are enabled to give it appropriate expression in their own place.

In some ways our world is closer to that of New Testament times than any age in between. That does not mean that the solutions then worked out are applicable now. It does mean that we are freer than our immediate forebears to tap those sources of creativity and imagination that carried the church from the time of Jesus to the crystallizing of its tradition some generations later. The difference may be expressed in the words of Ecclesiastes: then it was a time to plant, now it is a time to pluck up what is planted; then a time to gather stones together, now a time to cast away stones; then a time to build up, now a time to break down; then a time to sew, now a time to rend; then a time to speak, now a time to keep silence.[20]

The likeness is in the faith that in that silence, and indeed while men have been occupied in the din of scheming and planning, the Holy Spirit of God is at work. For it is not ultimately in the Church that Christians declare their belief, but 'in the Holy Spirit in the Holy Church'.[21]

NOTES

1. Cf. my quotation from John Knox on pp. 97f.

2. Athanasius, *On the Incarnation*, 24; cf. also John 19.36; and contrast with this the dubious theology sometimes heard today which likens the divisions of Christianity to the 'broken body of Christ on the cross'.

3. Cf. Eph. 1.9 f.; 3.9 f.; 4.4–6; and J. Knox, *op. cit.*, pp. 104–9.

4. Cf. Matt. 11.27; John 3.35; 5.20; 13.3.

5. Cf. John 13.20; 15.16; 20.23.

6. Cf. p. 99.

7. Cf. also Mark 3.14 f.; 6.7–13; Matt. 9.37–10.1, 5–15; Luke 6.12 f.; 9.1–5; 10.1–12, 16; and J. Knox, *op. cit.*, pp. 110–12.

8. Cf. pp. 87f.

9. Cyprian, *On the Unity of the Catholic Church*, 4 f.

10. J. Knox, *op. cit.*, p. 127.

11. Inaugurated in 1947 by a union of Anglicans, Methodists, Presbyterians, Congregationalists, Reformed and Lutheran churches, on the basis of an episcopal constitution. Negotiations started in 1919.

122

12. Stephen Neill, *The Church and Christian Union* (London: Oxford University Press, 1968), p. 402.

13. *Unity begins at Home* (London: SCM Press, 1964), p. 75.

14. John Huxtable, *Christian Unity, Some of the Issues* (London: Independent Press, 1966), p. 50.

15. Laurence Bright, O.P., 'Proposals for Teaching Theology in an English University', in J. Coulson (ed.), *Theology and the University* (London: Darton, Longman & Todd, 1964), pp. 277 f.

16. Hans Küng, *The Council and Reunion*, p. 172.

17. *The Sunday Times*, 6th October, 1968.

18. Cf. Chapter 5, note 10.

19. Cf. Chapter 7, note 3.

20. Cf. Eccles. 3.1–8.

21. Cf. H. Küng, *The Church*, pp. 30 ff.

Bibliography

J. V. Taylor, *The Primal Vision* (London: SCM Press, 1963).

Hans Küng, *The Church* (London: Burns & Oates, 1968).

A. M. Ramsey, *The Gospel and the Catholic Church* (London: Longmans, 1936).

John Knox, *The Early Church and the Coming Great Church* (New York: Abingdon Press, 1955 and London: Epworth, 1957).

E. L. Mascall, *Corpus Christi* (London: Longmans, 1965, Second edition).

Stephen Neill, *The Church and Christian Union* (London and New York: Oxford University Press, 1968).

Harvey Cox, *On Not Leaving It to the Snake* (New York: Macmillan, and London: SCM Press, 1968).

Robert Adolfs, *The Grave of God: Has the Church a Future?* (London: Burns & Oates, 1967).

David Martin, *A Sociology of English Religion* (London: SCM Press, and New York: Basic Books, 1967).
The Religious and the Secular (London: Routledge, 1969).

F. Boulard, *An Introduction to Religious Sociology: Pioneer Work in France* (London: Darton, Longman & Todd, 1960).

Index of Names

Index of Subjects

127

Chapter 31

eila shifted uncomfortably. She'd been waiting out-
le South Precinct for almost two hours. Evan Hill, the
in charge of the investigation into Richard Cutter's
d refused to see her, and the duty sergeant had forced
ive the building, so she'd picked a spot on Myrtle
the car park gate that allowed her to keep an eye on
ing's entrance and the vehicles coming and going.
d against a sign protruding from the verge, which
ice Only', and tried to take the weight off her legs.
uncomfortably humid afternoon and she was feel-
ull effects of her journey and her long vigil outside
n. She paced every few minutes in a vain attempt to
pain and fatigue from her legs, and tried to keep her
upied by watching the children's soccer match being
the pitch opposite the station.
Precinct was located in a residential neighbourhood
e Leila think of England. The pitch was a rich green
surrounded by large trees. Through their branches,
h golden leaves, Leila caught glimpses of charming
land-style houses on the other side of the pitches.
e grew bored of watching the game, Leila counted
ng overhead, kept a tally of red cars versus blue, and
uess the life stories of the people filing in and out

Chapter 30

Pearce hung up. The improvements Leila had made to
her Ghostlink communicator meant they could use them in
public with little fear of anyone realizing they weren't mobile
phones. The devices permitted encrypted satellite communication almost anywhere in the world, and Pearce was certain
Leila could have made a small fortune if she'd sold the tech-
nology, but she'd opted to keep its existence secret. The
Ghostlinks were for their exclusive use.

'Mr Martin will see you now,' the receptionist said.

Pearce was in the lobby of the Seattle Port Authority building, waiting to see Richard Cutter's boss, Harry Martin. Pearce
followed the receptionist out of the charmless corporate waiting area, through a security door into the corridor beyond.

Small offices lay either side. Most featured an administrator
at a desk, surrounded by stacks of paperwork. The receptionist led Pearce through the building, up a couple of flights of
stairs onto the executive floor. The Director of Operations'
office was located in the north-west corner of the block.

'Mr . . . er?' Martin asked, rising from behind his large
desk.

'Samuels,' Pearce replied. 'Thanks for seeing me,' he added,
shaking the man's hand.

'Thanks, Ken,' Harry said to the receptionist, who shut

the door behind him when he withdrew. Harry turned his attention to Pearce. 'Have a seat. What can I do for you, Mr Samuels?'

'I'm with the *Daily Star* in London,' Pearce lied. 'I was hoping to talk to friends of Richard Cutter.'

Harry immediately became defensive and his smile dropped. 'You told Ken you were here to talk about the port.'

'Would you have agreed to see me?' Pearce countered.

'We're all saddened by what happed to Richie. Most of us just want to move on,' Harry replied.

'I understand, but this idea of a Midas Killer, well, it's captured our readers' imaginations. I'd like to talk to people who might have seen Mr Cutter that day.'

'I don't think anyone here will have anything to say to you,' Harry said flatly. 'We're all pretty grossed out by the tabloid sensation. Let me show you out, Mr Samuels.'

Pearce felt sorry for Harry Martin. He could sense the man's anger at being deceived and his disapproval of the salacious angle Pearce was taking over his colleague's death, but he was still managing to be cordial. It showed real character, and Pearce didn't want to cause a good man any more pain. He'd try the bar where Richard Cutter died and canvas the staff and patrons for anything on who might have killed him.

'Sure,' Pearce said. 'Sorry to have troubled you.'

He followed Martin downstairs into the ground-floor corridor. His heart pounded out a couple of thunderous beats and it took every ounce of discipline to control the fight or flight response provoked by what he saw ahead of him. There, coming along the corridor, was one of the men who'd escaped from Al Aqarab prison.

'Hey, Harry,' the man said as he passed.

'Hey, Zee,' Harry replied. 'You g[o] to talk about the *Elite*.'

'Drop by anytime,' the escapee s

The man walked on and so di[d] his mind a jumble of questions. Th this dangerous wanted man was w Authority.

'You OK?' Harry asked, waitin[g] security door.

'Yes, sorry,' Pearce replied, hur[r] breath and tried to calm the rising

He'd just caught a huge break.

of the modern precinct building. But the distractions always led to the same place: Hannan. No matter what Leila did, she always found herself thinking about her older sister, wondering whether she was still alive, where she was, and who she might be with. And when those questions had been dwelt on, and finally passed through her mind unanswered, Leila always wound up at the same low place, feeling an overwhelming sense of guilt that she was here on Huxley Blaine Carter's errand, rather than on the trail of the last surviving member of her family.

Movement caught Leila's eye through the high perimeter fence and she was grateful to see Detective Evan Hill emerge from the precinct building and cross the car park to a dark-blue SUV. She recognized the grizzled, experienced police officer from a photo in a newspaper report about a prior investigation. She pushed herself off the 'Police Only' sign, limped over to the sidewalk by the gates and waited patiently as he reversed his car out of its space and drove towards her. As he slowed to a stop and waited for the gate to retract, he caught sight of Leila and eyed her with unmistakeable suspicion. When he drove through the gate and stopped at the intersection with Myrtle Street, Leila approached the car and tapped on his window.

He lowered it.

'Yeah?'

Up close, Leila could see the grey-haired man had the hard eyes and palpable cynicism of someone who'd seen too much of life's darkness, and when she looked down, she saw his right hand was wrapped around a pistol that rested on the passenger seat.

'My name is Maria Grattan. I'm foreign correspondent with *Il Giustizia*, we're an Italian security publication.'

'I know who you are,' Hill said. 'I didn't want to see you before, and I don't want to see you now.'

'I'm interested in the Richard Cutter investigation,' Leila pressed.

'There is no investigation,' Hill replied. 'The chief got some faulty intel and I got bounced into paying lip service. Richard Cutter died of natural causes. This Midas thing is pure sensation to sell newspapers.'

'I'm not so sure,' Leila said. 'I thought we might be able to share information.'

'I know how that plays. I give you information and you don't share jack shit with me.'

'We could—' Leila began, but Hill cut her off.

'Save your breath, lady.' He pulled onto Myrtle Street and sped away.

Leila cursed inwardly, doubly angry at the pain she'd endured waiting for a man who'd given her nothing. She heard a low tri-tone and pulled her Ghostlink from her pocket.

'Go ahead,' she said.

'*I'm going to give you an address*,' Pearce told her. '*Get here as soon as you can.*'

Chapter 32

Less than an hour later, Leila turned onto Kenyon Street, a run-down road in a rough neighbourhood called South Park. She found Pearce near the corner, crouched beside his motorbike. He had the seat off and looked as though he was making repairs. Leila parked behind the R1 and lowered the window as he came over.

'Fifty metres up, on the right,' Pearce said. 'Small wooden house. Green paint.'

Leila glanced along the street. Poverty wasn't hidden here. It was evident in the old rusty cars, missing roof tiles, broken guttering and overgrown yards. She spotted the house Pearce was referring to – one of the most derelict of all.

'Got it,' she said.

'Our target is inside.'

'You're kidding me!'

'I saw him at the port authority. Walked right past him. He works there,' Pearce said. 'His real name is Ziad Malek. He's a shift supervisor. Replaced the guy who died, Richard Cutter.'

'You think they killed Cutter? Why would anyone murder someone to get a job like that?' Leila asked.

'He's in there with the getaway driver from the prison break.'

'We should bring them in,' Leila said, suddenly thinking about her own sister. If the man they were looking for was in that house, her work was done. They could apprehend him and extract whatever information Blaine Carter needed.

'I know what you're thinking,' Pearce replied. 'If we bring them in, who knows what we'll get? But we can be certain that any network around them will pack up and disappear. If we keep them in play, we might get to whoever's pulling the strings.'

Leila felt her stomach tighten with frustration. 'We should take them now. There's no guarantee anyone else is involved.' Her words carried no conviction. Leila knew Pearce was right, that there were others, not least the man who'd broken out of Al Aqarab with Ziad Malek, but she was desperate to get on her sister's trail.

'Any sign of the other escapee?' she asked.

Pearce shook his head. 'We need to stay on these two until we know more.'

Leila nodded grudgingly.

'Have you got any gear with you?'

Pearce was referring to the equipment that had been in the flight cases Robert Clifton had delivered to their unusual apartment.

'Just a basic kit,' Leila replied. 'A couple of cameras, trackers and bugs.' She climbed out of the Yukon and went to the boot. She opened it and showed Pearce the contents of a Peli Storm flight case that wasn't much bigger than a shoebox. The electronics gear she'd mentioned was encased in laser-cut foam.

'Can you set the camera for motion?' Pearce asked.

Leila checked for any passers-by, but the street was deserted.

She switched on the tablet that controlled the devices and adjusted the camera's settings, while Pearce pocketed a tracker and a bug.

'We'll have to come back to rig the house,' Pearce said. 'But I can set up the camera to let us know when they're out. It will also pick up any visitors. I can rig the car to give us ears on them and tell us where they go.'

Leila handed Pearce the tiny buttonhole camera. 'Do you need a mount?'

'Some putty,' he replied.

Leila handed him a tube of fast-drying modelling cement, and he set off down the street. She shut the boot, climbed behind the wheel and started the engine. She watched him intently, ready to step on the accelerator if anything went wrong.

Chapter 33

Pearce walked down the street, careful not to move too fast or too slow, both of which would have made him memorable for any casual observers. He squeezed a pea-sized quantity of modelling cement and shaped it around the base of the buttonhole camera. He was about twenty metres from the house where Ziad Malek and Narong Angsakul were holed up when he saw movement at the window. The Thai man crossed the front room and crouched down for a moment before returning to wherever he'd come from. His baggy shorts, vest and wild long hair marked him out as a climber or surfer. Only the tattoos that covered his muscular body hinted at villainy: Pearce recognized one, a spider's web, as a Thai time-served marker.

Pearce kept walking until he was almost directly opposite the house. There was a telegraph pole on his side of the street and he crouched beside it and pretended he was tying his laces. He pushed the buttonhole camera against the wooden pole, above a metal junction box, and positioned it to face the small green house opposite. Satisfied it was secure and no more noticeable than a bit of dirt stuck to some gum, Pearce got to his feet and hurried across the street towards a Buick that was more relic than car.

The tracker was easy. Slightly larger than a ten-pence piece, he slipped the magnetic wafer inside the rear wheel arch and felt it stick to the chassis with a satisfying click. The listening device would be more difficult. Pearce was reaching for the nearest door handle when he quickly crouched. Angsakul was moving again. He must have sensed something, because he came to the window and looked at the car. Pearce chanced a look towards the house, and saw the grim-faced killer scan the front yard. After a moment, Angsakul turned his attention to something else – possibly the TV – and then receded from sight.

Pearce was in a risky position and wanted out quickly. If he was discovered, there was a real likelihood of violence and he also risked blowing the investigation by alerting Angsakul and Ziad to the fact they'd been found. Pearce tried the nearest handle – locked. The Buick was old enough not to have central locking, so he moved round the car, trying the others, and discovered they were all locked, but he was relieved when the boot popped open. It wasn't ideal, but it was the best he could do under the circumstances. He put the listening device beneath the oily carpet, positioning it as close to the rear seats as possible. He replaced the carpet, closed the boot and quickly moved away from the house, continuing his walk west, away from Leila.

Pearce glanced over his shoulder every so often, but saw no sign his presence had been detected. A couple of dishevelled-looking men staggered out of the house opposite and slumped on the porch steps, clutching half-drunk bottles of beer. Pearce had been lucky with his timing.

When he was out of sight of the house, he picked up his pace and within five minutes had circled the block and was reunited with Leila. She was in her large SUV and had the engine running, and didn't notice him approach from behind.

'We won't need that quick getaway,' he said, startling her.

'*Ya hayawan!*' she exclaimed, calling him an animal in the most affectionate tone.

'We're set,' Pearce said. 'Let's not push our luck here. I'll see you at the flat.'

He jumped on his motorbike and pressed the ignition as Leila pulled away. The bike roared to life and within moments he was speeding west.

Chapter 34

Few can see beyond the edges of their own experiences, Elroy thought as he sat in the back of the police car parked on Horton Street. It was how he and the people he worked with thrived, by operating outside the margins, doing things most would consider impossible. Scientists spend years searching for cures. Politicians devote decades to attaining power. Artists a lifetime pursuing success. Why did so few realize that same dedication was applied to what he did? If a prize was sufficiently big, someone would invest the time and effort required to attain it.

The plan was unfolding better than expected. Ziad Malek, the second-generation immigrant, had been easy to radicalize. The setbacks he'd experienced had left him vulnerable, and his heart had hardened against the people who had betrayed him. As always, the petty criminal with a flexible approach to morality had quickly accepted the logic of stepping out-side the law for retribution. Elroy had been surprised by how untroubled Ziad had been by murder. Either he was hiding it well, or his hate and anger had silenced his conscience. Elroy's initial assessment of the man had been of someone more humane, softer, and he'd expected to have to do more coaxing.

Eddie and Kirsty Fletcher, the husband and wife psychopaths

who led the local chapter of the Red Wolves, were blinded by promises of riches and power, and had kept up their end of the bargain, bringing connections with the men who sat in the front of the police car. They too were motivated by greed, and it surprised Elroy how unimaginative people were, as if money was the only thing that mattered. They never saw the bigger truth that lay beyond the dollar bills.

Ziad had given them the consignment details and one of Fletcher's men had been posted to keep watch on Jefferson National Trucking, the transportation company that was ultimately owned and controlled by Rasul Salamov. Jefferson National ran three big rigs and employed five contract drivers, and when the spy had contacted Fletcher and told him the identity of the driver who'd be collecting the consignment, Elroy had been very pleased. The container would be collected by Jake Lowell, an ex-con with a substance abuse problem, a man who could quite plausibly have formed an alliance with the East Hill Mob – a rival outfit to the Salamovs.

Elroy heard the low rumble of a large engine and saw the lights of a big rig flare as it turned right off Marginal Way. The eighteen-wheel truck rumbled slowly onto Horton Street, and drove beneath the highway overpass that dominated the western end of the road. They were less than a mile from the port, but it was late and Horton Street was devoid of traffic. Elroy could see the lights of vehicles on the Highway 99 overpass, but none of the drivers would see what was happening beneath it.

'Go,' Elroy said, and the police car shot forward.

Another car parked on the other side of the road surged towards the truck, and Elroy saw the uniformed driver and his passenger pull down their ski masks to cover their faces.

Elroy and the men in his car did likewise as the big rig came to a shuddering halt. The police cars blocked the vehicle's way beneath the eastern edge of the overpass.

The two men in the front of the car stepped out, and Elroy watched as one drew his weapon and covered his partner, who approached the truck.

'Get out! Get out now!' the man with the gun yelled.

Elroy had wanted them to use police-issue pistols, but Fletcher had told him the dirty cops on their payroll preferred MP5s for their out of hours work. The MP5 was a nasty little gun favoured by people who like to make a lot of mess, but Elroy didn't think the decision worth fighting.

The gunman opened fire and a volley of bullets chewed the asphalt around the truck, the noise echoing beneath the overpass.

'Get out!' the man shouted again.

The masked men from the other car were also out, and they both brandished their machine guns in the direction of the truck.

Jake Lowell looked every bit the dishevelled oxy addict as he hauled himself out of the cab. He clambered down the steps and stumbled nervously as he reached the road.

'Go,' the shooter instructed, and his masked colleague pushed past Jake and climbed into the truck.

The shooter glanced at Elroy, who nodded. No witnesses. The truth had to be kept a mystery. No one would miss Jake Lowell, not even his estranged teenage daughter.

The shooter turned to face Jake, who was walking forward with his hands raised.

'Take it. I don't care,' he said. 'I'm just the driver, and I never saw your—'

Jake was cut off by a volley of bullets hitting him in the abdomen. Elroy saw the familiar look of horror and disbelief common to most people when they realize death is upon them.

Jake took a step forward and survived another heartbeat before his eyes went blank and he toppled over, dead.

The shooter returned to the car, tossed his gun on the passenger seat, and slid behind the wheel.

The other car pulled a U-turn and headed east on Horton Street. Elroy's driver followed, trailed by the large, lumbering truck which traced a crescent to avoid Jake's body.

Elroy felt a flash of satisfaction. They'd successfully concluded a critical part of their plan. His next move was to go to China to ensure they capitalized on the opportunity their success would create.

Part Two

Part Two

Chapter 35

She'd been known as Brigitte Attali for years, but the name still didn't fit. Perhaps it was permeated with the hatred and anger of the groups she'd infiltrated as an agent of the DGSE; first the *Crois-de-Feux*, then Progress Britain. She was all too familiar with the snarling lips, fiery eyes and red faces of hate. As someone with albinism, she'd drawn animosity and derision for being different throughout her life, but the far-right extremists had welcomed her and embraced her condition as a visible sign of her racial purity. Perhaps it was their idiotic view of her genetics that had tainted the name; it would forever be associated with her acceptance by the peddlers of hate.

'So what do you want to discuss, Chloe?'

She hadn't used her real name, Chloe Duval, for so long, and was surprised when Echo said it. They'd known each other in Paris, long before Brigitte Attali had been born.

They were in a busy restaurant fifteen minutes' walk from the bugged apartment. It was a place that took health seriously and Brigitte had been subjected to a rapid virus and temperature check before she'd been allowed inside. She was the only foreigner in the place, which was alive with the buzz of conversation, the clatter of dishes and shouts from the kitchen and waiting staff. It was wild and chaotic, but the food smelled delicious. All around them people dunked meats into their hotpots, cooking at their tables and filling the busy room with rich aromas.

'Who are you working for?' Brigitte asked, leaning across the empty table.

'I told you,' Echo replied. 'We manufacture—'

Brigitte cut her off. 'My friend and I took a walk today. We went to explore the industrial district.' She and Wollerton had decided the only way to conceal their intentions while they were under surveillance was to visit a number of factories, so that Qingdao Consumer Products would simply be one of many places they were interested in. They'd started the day by attempting to lose the two men who followed them from their apartment, but it became apparent they were the subjects of a much more comprehensive operation. They lost the first two tails, but became aware of a third, and when they'd shaken her, a fourth, fifth and sixth. Brigitte suspected aerial support, possibly satellite, or a tracker hidden in their clothing. She'd lost count of the number of people who'd brushed past her as they walked the busy streets of Qingdao. She and Wollerton had agreed they couldn't proceed any further under the circumstances. Attempting to infiltrate the factory or question its employees would reveal their true intentions and put their mission at risk, so Brigitte had persuaded Wollerton to let her invite Echo out to dinner alone.

'We were followed,' Brigitte continued, 'and we found some artefacts in the apartment.'

Echo smiled wryly, and the mask of innocence fell away.

'So I want to know who you're working for.'

'Why?' Echo asked.

'You want the truth? Or do you want to keep playing this bullshit game?'

'As you prefer,' Echo replied.

'I'm tired,' Brigitte said. 'I've spent too long in the shadows, trying to outsmart people like you, pretending to be friends with scum . . .'

Echo scoffed.

'Other scum, not you,' Brigitte remarked.

'Thank you,' Echo said sarcastically.

'During my last operation,' Brigitte hesitated, 'I . . . I was going to murder an innocent man to get closer to my object-ive. This job . . . you know what it does to us.'

Echo nodded sombrely.

'And for all my service and sacrifice, what did I get? Ejected from Mortier for one perceived failing,' Brigitte said, recalling her dismissal from the service's HQ. 'I want out. I'm finished with this life. I've had enough of powerful men sending me to face death. So if you're working for your old employer, we don't have a lot to talk about. But if you're in the private sector and can access funds, we can continue.'

Brigitte leaned back as a waiter deposited their order on the table; a medley of roasted meats, rice and vegetables. It smelled delicious, but Brigitte had lost her appetite. Of all the questionable things she'd done in her life, this was one of the most difficult. She wasn't just gambling her own life; she was risking someone else's.

'Continue,' Echo said, once the waiter withdrew.

'OK,' Brigitte replied. 'We're here to investigate a factory.'

'Which one?'

'Qingdao Consumer Products.'

Echo's eyes lit up with unmistakeable recognition. 'Why?'

'We found a chip in a device used in a prison escape. It was made there,' Brigitte replied.

'Who's we?'

'I don't know. I'm just a drone, hired for a fee,' Brigitte said. 'The factory is yours?'

'It belongs to people I know,' Echo responded.

'Who are?'

'Do you really want this?'

'I want out,' Brigitte reiterated. There was truth in her words. Her life was wearing thin, and ever since she'd started working for Blaine Carter, she'd questioned where she was going. She'd joined the DGSE out of a sense of patriotism, but the light of honour had been extinguished by the dark things she'd seen and done, and now she didn't have the memory of her intentions to cling to. She was a mercenary.

'Are you sure?' Echo asked. 'These people . . .' She tailed off.

'What?' Brigitte asked.

'I have a husband and two children,' Echo said hesitantly. Was she crying? 'Certain decisions aren't ours to make.' Had she just admitted she was being blackmailed by her new employers? Were they using the lives of her family as leverage? Such things were commonplace in their world, which was why Brigitte had chosen to travel through life without any baggage.

'I want money,' Brigitte said. 'Enough to retire on.'

'And in return?'

'I'll give you the people I'm working for, starting with the man I'm with.' Brigitte thought of Wollerton pacing the apartment, trusting her to do the right thing. She hadn't told him what she had planned, because there was no way he would have sanctioned it.

'How much?' Echo asked.

'Four million euros.'

Echo glanced away, and Brigitte followed her eye line to see two men who looked like street thugs, seated at a table across the room. One of the men nodded.

'We will pay that on the condition your companion is able to identify your ultimate employer,' Echo said.

Four million for Blaine Carter's name? Brigitte wondered exactly what the Silicon Valley billionaire had drawn them into.

'No,' Brigitte said. 'Half up front, sent to a Cayman bank.'

Echo checked with the men, who were obviously her superiors. 'OK.'

Two million just for the prospect of learning Blaine Carter's name. He can't have been honest about who he really was and what he'd hired them to do. There had to be more to it. Was Blaine Carter working for someone else? Brigitte was glad she'd presented herself as an ignorant foot soldier. Ignorance was probably the only thing that stopped the two men trying to drag her off to be tortured in some dark place. That and her reputation. She had no doubt Echo would have fully briefed them on who they were up against.

'When I've received confirmation the money has been transferred, I'll drug him,' Brigitte said, and her stomach twisted into a knot at the thought of dosing Wollerton. 'Come at night. I'll help you take him.'

Chapter 36

Pearce could see it in the way she lingered. Moments too long to reply, seconds spent drifting in thought before suddenly recalling what she was doing. In anyone else, these might have been early signs of a neurological disorder, but Pearce knew the cause of Leila's distraction. She was wrestling with the thought of her sister being out there somewhere, and trying to come to terms with her guilt at not racing to pick up her tail. He wouldn't have blamed her if she'd abandoned the assignment. Family was family after all, and unlike his own parents, Leila hadn't given up on her kin. But she was a woman of principle and was also smart enough to know she stood a better chance of finding Hannan with Huxley Blaine Carter's help.

Pearce crossed the road opposite their building, carrying two cups of coffee – his with cream and sugar, hers unadulterated. They were in the heart of Seattle in a thriving neighbourhood full of shops, restaurants, hotels and office blocks. People thronged the streets, particularly around the pedestrianized zones that offered a view of the bay, but in a mark of how much life had changed since the pandemic, they generally took great care to keep a safe distance from each other. Pearce picked his way through one such widely dispersed crowd and entered the building. The security guard and receptionist accepted his presence without question. One of Blaine Carter's people must have briefed them about the new tenants on the fifteenth floor. He rode the private elevator and stepped into the vast open-plan space to find Leila where he'd left her; hunched over a computer at the desk she'd claimed as her own. The other desk was covered in gear from the flight cases Robert Clifton had provided.

'White, six sugars,' Pearce said, putting the coffee down beside Leila.

She smiled. 'You know what would happen if you gave me something so disgusting? It's better you never find out,' she said. 'Have you seen the news?'

She turned her laptop so Pearce could see the screen, which displayed a *Seattle Star* article. The headline read, 'Man Shot Dead at Seattle Port'.

'A trucker was murdered last night,' Leila said. 'His vehicle was stolen.'

'Our targets involved?' Pearce asked.

Leila shook her head. 'Neither of them left the house.'

She switched to another window which broadcast live footage from the buttonhole camera Pearce had installed on Kenyon Street.

'I reviewed last night's footage,' she said. 'Couple of passing cars, a resident walking a dog. Couple of passing drunks staggering along the street. Nobody went in or came out of the target house.'

'You get anything on Malek?' Pearce asked.

Leila nodded. 'Only child of Hosni and Falak Malek, residents of Cleveland, Ohio. Pulled in on a few misdemeanours as a teenager, but no record since then. He's one of the smart ones. Too cunning to get caught.'

'Except in Egypt,' Pearce remarked.

Leila handed Pearce a sheaf of papers; port person-
nel records, school transcripts, official state and federal
documents – everything she'd found on Ziad Malek. It was
pretty standard stuff, and didn't mark him out as a dangerous
international criminal.

'And Angsakul?' he asked.

'*Wala haga*,' Leila replied. *Nothing*. 'I can tell you he exists,
because I've seen him, but as far as a digital footprint goes,
he's a ghost.'

Pearce thought for a moment. 'Ziad needs his identity for
his job at the port. His employment creates records—'

'Yeah,' Leila cut in. 'He had the same job before he was
arrested in Egypt.'

'So they broke him out to get his old job back,' Pearce
observed. 'A false ID would have been pointless, so they
couldn't entirely wipe his digital presence like they have with
Angsakul.'

'Right,' Leila agreed. 'Just remove any photos to prevent
people like us running a recognition programme that would
link Ziad Malek, the port employee, to Ibrahim Mahmood,
the prisoner who escaped from Al Aqarab.'

'If we find out why they wanted . . .' Pearce fell silent as
he registered movement on screen. Ziad Malek left the house
and walked to the old Buick.

'He's on the move,' Pearce observed.

'Can't be work. I pulled the rota and he's on the late shift
today,' Leila said.

'They might have called him in because of the killing.'

They watched Ziad drive out of shot.

'I'm going to follow him,' Pearce said, 'find out where he's going.'

His attention was drawn back to the screen when a Ducati Scrambler stopped in front of the house. Narong Angsakul emerged in jeans and a leather jacket, helmet in hand. He mounted the bike, put his helmet on and tapped the unidentified rider's lid to signal he was ready. The motorcyclist kicked into gear and the bike left frame.

'I'm going over there first,' Pearce said. 'We need to bug the house.'

Leila looked at him with disdain. 'Let me know when you'll be back. I'll have your pipe and slippers waiting and a nice home cooked meal, *ya ghabi*,' she said, calling him an idiot. 'Malek could have met twenty people in the time it takes you to rig that house properly. I'll do it. You stay with Malek.'

Pearce smiled. 'And if I argue?'

'It'll be worse than if you'd brought me a coffee with milk and six sugars,' she replied with a sardonic smile. 'I'll be fine, Scott. I know how to take care of myself. Get out of here,' she commanded.

Pearce nodded, grabbed his gear, and hurried to intercept his target.

Chapter 37

This was the dangerous part. Ziad had been summoned and knew what he'd face. He parked outside the community centre and tried to still his thundering heart as he crossed the lot and went inside the Haqeeq Bookstore. A soft tone sounded and the manager peered out from behind a rack of shelves and nodded a sombre greeting. He tested Ziad for coronavirus, and when he saw the negative result gestured towards the back of the shop. As he walked on, Ziad took a moment to calm himself. If Deni Salamov saw him like this, he'd assume guilt, and Ziad had no intention of giving up the game so easily. He'd endured the pain of Al Aqarab, the misery of betrayal, and the loss of Essi, and the thought of all he'd suffered stirred his anger. He pictured Essi in the arms of her new lover, and imagined Deni and Rasul laughing at how easily they'd framed Ziad. The fury burned away any nervousness, and when he turned and crossed the shop, he was calm, like the eye of a storm. Deni, Rasul and the old man Abbas Idrisov, the Abacus, were seated in the small reading area at the back of the shop, and with them were Osman, Ilman and Surkho, three of Deni's most fearsome enforcers. They were big, brutish men who relished any opportunity for violence. They stood in the corner and watched Ziad with hungry eyes.

If there was ugly business to be done today, they were eager to get to it.

'Have a seat,' Deni said coldly. No greeting. No pretence.

Ziad took the unoccupied chair between Rasul and Abacus, and Deni fixed him with a hard stare. The silent shop seemed to press in on them.

'What's going on?' Ziad asked.

'We lost a shipment last night,' Deni replied.

'Lost?' Rasul said angrily. 'It was stolen and my driver was killed.'

'Stolen?' Ziad responded. He paused, playing up the moment of realization. 'And you think I was involved?'

The suggestion was met with silence.

'Show him,' Deni said, and Abacus picked up an iPad that was resting on the table between them.

'The police released this,' the old man said as he played a video.

Ziad watched traffic camera footage of distant activity. Taken from a hundred yards away, the video showed two police cars blocking a street that ran beneath an overpass. Ziad recognized it as Horton Street, a cut-through a short distance from the port. Whatever had happened beneath the bridge was beyond the camera's view, but after a few moments he saw three police officers get in the cars and drive away, followed by the big rig.

'This wasn't street gangsters,' Abacus remarked as he set the iPad on the table.

'It was planned,' Deni agreed. 'By people who knew exactly when the rig was coming out.'

All three men looked at Ziad pointedly, and he grew very aware of Osman and the other two, standing in the corner, waiting to be let off the leash.

'Why would I do this?' Ziad asked. 'And how? You have blessed me by giving me my old life. Why would I endanger that? And I didn't know when the truck would be coming,' he protested. 'I give Rasul the container codes, but he's responsible for arranging pick-up. I couldn't have known when he'd choose to move the shipment.' *But the people I'm working with, who have his depot under surveillance, would know,* Ziad thought.

Deni looked at Rasul, who nodded sheepishly.

'Even if I'd wanted to, I couldn't have arranged such a thing, *wa Allahi al azeem,*' Ziad said, adding an oath swearing his honesty in the name of God.

'Who knew the time of collection?' Deni asked Rasul.

'No one,' Rasul replied, fixing Ziad with a suspicious look.

'Except the port scheduler,' Ziad observed. 'Your driver would have to give notice of his arrival so the container and loaders would be ready. And who knows how many people that schedule gets sent to. If someone has managed to infiltrate the port . . .' he left the suggestion hanging.

'I want you to bring us a list of names,' Deni said. 'Everyone who knew about the collection.'

'What do we do about the Italians?' Rasul asked.

The Cresci family, headed by Ben Cresci, were among Deni's biggest customers. This would have been a large, valuable shipment. Cagey and distrustful, Cresci didn't take disappointment well.

Deni shifted uncomfortably. 'They've given us seven days to make good.'

Abacus whistled.

'Shit,' Rasul said. 'That's not long enough to bring over another shipment. You need to get more time.'

Ziad was shocked by the suddenness and ferocity of the slap. Deni smacked his son so hard it made Abacus gasp.

'Never tell me what to do!' Deni yelled at his son. 'We're lucky we're not already dead. This has brought a lot of police attention and made us look like fucking amateurs.'

Rasul blushed furiously and his eyes burned with murderous anger, but he had the good sense to stay quiet.

'I know a man,' Ziad said. 'I met him in Al Aqarab . . .'

'The man you're living with?' Deni asked.

Ziad was surprised, but he shouldn't have been; Deni was a cunning old fox who'd built an empire by being careful. He'd have checked Ziad out, but did he have the house under constant surveillance? Had he seen Elroy? The American came and went at odd times. Ziad forced himself to remain calm. If Deni had evidence of his treachery, he'd already be dead. 'Yes. He's name's Awut and he has contacts in China. He claims to be able to access product. Opiates.'

'Synthetic?' Deni said.

Ziad nodded.

'We never touched that shit,' Deni responded testily, but Ziad sensed disagreement from Abacus and Rasul. 'I've seen what it does. The Afghan spice is bad enough,' Deni said, using his euphemism for heroin, 'but with these synthetics, people have no chance.'

An ethical drug dealer, Ziad thought wryly, but he knew better. The man was simply afraid of innovation he didn't understand.

'But we have so little time,' Abacus remarked. 'Perhaps this once—'

'No,' Deni said.

'I don't understand,' Ziad ventured. 'We supply heroin,' he

noted Deni's flash of anger at his use of the word, 'but we won't sell products that are almost exactly the same, but far more profitable. I think you're being too protective of the *kafir*.'

The Arabic word for infidel had the desired effect. Abacus and Rasul looked puzzled and the three thugs looming in the corner leaned a little closer.

Deni scoffed. '*Kafir*? Are you a religious man now?'

Ziad nodded. 'I met a man in Al Aqarab, a religious man, a great sheikh,' he lied. 'He taught me jihad isn't just about observance and piety, or guns and bombs. It is about fighting the *kafir* by any means. You may not know it, but Allah smiles on what you do,' he said, getting into the flow. He'd heard enough hypocritical, twisted pious rants in Al Aqarab to have no shortage of material. 'You sell product that is targeted at those who do not follow the Quran. Your customers are drug addicts and criminals. Abusers of themselves and others. Debasers of all. Your product finds them and kills them. Slowly, but surely. Perhaps you've never seen it in this light, but you are a servant of jihad.'

Abacus nodded, and Ziad looked up to see the three men who would have gladly killed him minutes ago signalling their agreement.

'Ha!' Rasul remarked. 'A philosopher.'

'If we are to engage in jihad,' Ziad said. 'What is one weapon when compared to another?'

Deni had the look of a man who'd picked up a stick only to find it was a venomous snake. This was not playing out as he'd expected. 'I am not engaged in jihad. I'm engaged in business, and my business isn't that shit.'

Ziad sensed disappointment from everyone else in the room. He'd given them a momentary glimpse of a cause, a